Constituencies and Leaders in Congress

Harvard Political Studies. Published under the direction of the Department of Government in Harvard University

John E. Jackson

Constituencies and Leaders in Congress

Their Effects on Senate Voting Behavior

Harvard University Press, Cambridge, Massachusetts, 1974

To my teachers: Nelson, Keith, Otto, Doug, and John

Acknowledgments

This study has received considerable encouragement and support from numerous individuals and organizations. They deserve many thanks and share no blame. Extensive discussions with and advice from Doug Price, John Kain, Eric Hanushek, and Ed Haefele have been particularly valuable. The extensive comments submitted by David Kovenock led to substantial improvement and prove, once again, that authors and reviewers are not adversaries. Finally, and certainly not least, Linda Higgins and Eileen Nielsen merit special thanks for their patience and good humor in typing and retyping numerous drafts.

Parts of this study have previously appeared in *American Political Science Review*, vol. 65, no. 2 (June 1971), *Structural Models in the Social Sciences*, Arthur S. Goldberger and O. Dudley Duncan, eds. (New York: Seminar Press, 1973), and *Public Policy*, vol. 22, no. 3 (Summer, 1974). I am grateful to these publishers for permission to use their copyrighted material.

Financial support has been provided, in part, by grants to Harvard University from Resources for the Future, the IBM Corporation, and the Economic Development Administration in the Department of Commerce (OER–015–G–66–1).

Contents

Tables

Constituencies and Leaders in Congress

[1] Legislative Behavior and the Determinants of Public Policy

EXPLANATIONS OF LEGISLATIVE VOTING DECISIONS

The question of why legislators vote as they do has always intrigued political scientists. Approaches to this question can usually be grouped into one of three categories, depending upon the writer's experiences, point of view, and methodology. These are the internal or organizational descriptions, the representational or constituency theories, and the individual or trusteeship explanations. The first stresses the power of specific individuals, the influence of formal and informal leaders, and the importance of specialized committees and individual expertise. The representational view emphasizes the importance of individual constituencies and district interest groups, while the last explanation focuses on the views and attitudes of the individual legislators themselves.

The Organizational Explanation

The organizational model has generally been advocated by people who take an institutional view of Congress and are concerned with studying and specifying how information and influence are transmitted and affect individual decisions. The methodology of these studies is based largely on participant observations and statistical analyses showing the similarities in the voting patterns of different legislators. There are several variants to this internal model, each emphasizing the importance of different legislators or political leaders in the decisions of individual senators and congressmen.

The first of the organizational models stresses the importance of the formal leaders. These formal positions are the elected party floor leaders and their whips and the chairmen and ranking minority members of each committee—the seniority leaders.[1] These studies start with descriptions of the powers of the various leadership positions and the capabilities of the individuals occupying them. The leaders' sources of influence, in addition to their general pursuasive abilities, are derived from their control over internal resources—committee assignments, office space, campaign funds, favors, the scheduling of legislation, and access to the president.[2] The party floor leader especially can use these resources to exchange for a particular vote at a crucial time or to obtain the allegiance of individual legislators who hope to receive favorable treatment from the party leader on personally important matters. The individual committee chairmen and minority leaders have influence because they are in positions to affect the content of legislation considered by their committees, even to the point of blocking a bill for an extended period of time.[3] Because legislators who are not members of a committee may have a strong interest in its decisions and deliberations, the committee leaders can trade their influence over committee decisions for these legislators' support on various pieces of legislation. For example, the chairman of the committee dealing with housing may be able to get a representative from an urban area to support the chairman's position on various bills in return for a particular piece of housing legislation. Truman has observed though that in most cases of conflict between floor leaders and seniority leaders, it is the floor leaders who are more influential.[4]

A variation on the organizational approach emphasizes the

importance of informal leaders. These people are important
because of the influence they have developed from their personal
expertise, experience, seniority, or simply because they are
members of some inner club or clique which as a group strongly
influences the body as a whole. William White's description of the
U.S. Senate as a club, with an inner elite group of members, and
Senator Clark's description of this same group as the "Senate
Establishment" are the best illustrations of this conception of the
legislature.[5] The membership of this establishment is described
as bipartisan and based largely on seniority and on being elected
from a one-party state. The establishment gets its influence from
its ability to control the committees and the important party
positions. These positions are then used to thwart attempts by
the president and the congressional majority to pass legislation
distasteful to the club members, who are generally more conservative than the rest of Congress. Access to the club is based in part
on willingness to go along with the existing establishment and
to support them on various issues. Clark, for example, points out
that the likelihood of receiving a preferred committee assignment
was substantially correlated with opposition to changes in the
cloture rule being advocated by liberals as a way to reduce the
power of southern Democrats.[6] The positions taken by club
members can also be influential in how votes are cast on substantive legislation.[7]

   By far the most formalized of the organizational views of the
legislature is presented by authors starting from the formal theories
of organizational behavior developed by social psychologists.[8]
In this view, legislatures are complex organizations faced with the
task of making decisions on an exceedingly wide range of quite
technical and complicated subjects. The response of most legislative bodies to the demands of these complex tasks has been to
encourage specialization among the members. The U.S. Congress
has committees dealing exclusively with military procurement,
housing, and welfare, and individual legislators become known as
specialists in each of these fields.

The complexity of most legislation being dealt with, the legislator's own efforts to master one or two areas, and the scarcity of available time combine to mean that most legislators do not and cannot develop the knowledge and information required to evaluate completely each bill and amendment put before them. Consequently, they come to rely on certain individuals or institutions, such as committee chairmen or other experts, to provide them with information on how to vote on most bills. This desired information may relate to how a bill will effect their constituency, the position of some special interests, or how it fits with their particular ideological position. In any case, these information sources, or cue-givers, become important determinants of how individual legislators will vote. These cue-givers are often the very individuals identified as important influences in the formal and informal leader explanations—the party leaders, whips, and seniority leaders on the committees, as well as the individual experts. As with the other organizational explanations, all these influences are derived from within the legislature, or at least from within the formal governmental structure if the president is included. External factors such as constituencies, interest groups, or the legislator's own preferences may be important in these models, but their influence comes only through a few cue sources, such as the party or committee leaders and is traced by determining which cue sources a legislator follows. These external influences are not used to explain or predict voting behavior of individual legislators.

The Representational Explanation

People who see legislatures as representative bodies argue that constituencies are an important influence on a legislator's behavior. The basic presumption of these models is that legislators are motivated by a desire to stay in office,[9] which requires that they consider the positions of their voting constituents and pursue voting strategies which will please a majority of these constituents. The simplest, and in many ways the most naïve, strategy suggested is for representatives to cast their votes on each issue the way a majority of their constituents would if they were voting on the bill.[10] By voting with the majority on each issue, legislators presumably increase their probability of reelection. That this majoritarian strategy will not guarantee reelection and may possibly insure the opposite has been discussed elsewhere.[11]

A more sophisticated view of the electorate recognizes that the people in most districts are far from homogenous with respect to their views on all issues. The political preference map of any district is a kaleidoscopic pattern of people with different preferences on various issues and varying levels of concern for each issue.[12] These issues may range from defense spending to full employment, to welfare reform, to public power. However, the importance of each will vary from one person to another, and the candidates' positions on the more salient issues will be more important in determining each person's voting decision. Thus, some people will vote primarily on the basis of the candidates' attitudes towards military spending, others on their willingness to accept inflation to reduce unemployment, a third group on the candidates' intentions to reform the welfare system, and so on.[13] The most rational electoral strategy in this case, in terms of winning elections, is for the representative to adopt positions which take account of these differences in concern and take non-majority positions on those issues where there is an intense minority. Depending upon the distributions of preferences and concerns, the candidate's positions predicted by this intensity model may be quite different from the positions predicted by the majoritarian model.[14] The legislators are still voting on the basis of constituency positions, however.

A still more sophisticated representational model also assumes that differences in opinions and concerns exist in the electorate and that politicians seek to accommodate them, but the accommodation process is more positive and aggressive than in the previous model. Representatives not only try to please the different minorities in their constituencies, but they try to use the issues that are not important to any of their constituents, which there-

fore have a small effect on their chances for reelection, to obtain
the support of other legislators for the positions that are important to their constituents.[15] This model assumes that the legislature
is always voting on some issues which are not considered important by any of the people in some district. Naturally which issues
are unimportant will vary from district to district. Thus, congressmen from western states where public power and general economic development are important issues will use their votes on
such issues as urban public housing, mass transit, and civil rights
to obtain the support of urban, industrial congressmen for irrigation, reclamation, and public power projects. In doing this trading,
legislators actively seek out other members who, because of their
constituents' interest in other issues, are willing to exchange votes
so that all legislators get bills passed which are of primary interest
to their own constituents. Haefele has even argued that these
trades will be the ones which the individual constituents would
make if they had the facilities and means to trade with all the
individual members of the other districts.[16] According to this
coalition model, each legislator is representing his constituency
but in a much more complex fashion than either of the simpler
representational models suggests.

A behavioral version of this coalition model suggests an important but alternative role for the political parties and their leaders.[17]
The party leaders' functions are to act as information clearinghouses and vote brokers. They try to ascertain the relative importance of different issues to each member and then build and
maintain the party coalition by negotiating the appropriate vote
trades. Individual members may end up voting with the majority
in their party or with their party leaders much of the time, but
they are doing so as part of the coalition. The party in this case
is an ongoing coalition built around a more or less stable set of
vote trades. The members of the party, either implicitly or explicitly, agree to support the types of legislation desired by
the different members of the party. However, they are still repre-

senting their constituents in the sense of the coalition model because the parties are the predicted coalition.

The difficulty in predicting legislators' voting behavior on the basis of constituency positions increases drastically as one moves from the majoritarian, to the issue saliency, and finally to the coalition model. In the case of the majoritarian model, one only needs to know where a majority of each legislator's constituents stand on each issue to predict what positions each legislator will take. With the issue saliency model, the constituency variables must also be able to measure the relative importance of each issue to the individual voter, how these saliencies relate to people's preferences on each issue, and finally what nonmajority positions are most likely to win elections. Thus, more information and a more elaborate electoral model are required to predict legislators' positions than in the simple majoritarian case. Finally, predicting legislators' positions by the coalition model requires information on the preferences of constituents and the salience of each issue not only for the single legislator, but for all legislators, because the predictions must take into account what trades are likely to be made. In all of these cases legislators are voting on the basis of influences from their constituents and not those of the internal legislative organization.

The Trusteeship Explanations

Finally, in the individual or trusteeship approach to legislative decision making, the legislature is seen as a forum where the merits and demerits of different policy proposals are debated, their consequences considered, and the important issues identified and resolved. The legislators themselves cast their votes on the basis of their own perceptions of the problem being considered and their assessment of what is "best" for the country. These perceptions and assessments are very dependent upon the experiences and philosophies of the individual legislators. Justifications for this model run all the way from statements by legislators that they feel their job is to act as trustees or statesmen to observations that this is the only way they can behave given the complexity of most issues and the conflicting or nonexistent demands of party leaders and constituencies.[18] This model requires fairly detailed knowledge of legislators' personal preferences, beliefs, and the consequences of the bills being considered to predict their voting behavior. A simplified version of this model has been called an ideological model by Matthews and Stimpson.[19] The difference between the ideological model and the larger trusteeship model is that the legislators' beliefs and preferences are assumed to follow some predetermined ideological pattern, such as a liberal or conservative dichotomy. Predictions of behavior then simply require a determination of the ideological orientation of the legislator and of the bill being considered.

PUBLIC POLICY AND MODELS OF LEGISLATIVE VOTING

The distinctions in these models, particularly with respect to how external demands influence legislation, are substantial, and the significance of their differences transcends discussion of how legislators make decisions. Each of the models is associated with different views on how legislatures *should* make decisions on national policy, on which outside influences *should* be considered in making these decisions, and on how best to insure that only these influences affect policy decisions.

The organizational model is more consistent with the notion that the country needs a "responsible party" system. The keystone of this party system is that each party, and presumably there will be two, should campaign on a distinct, national platform adopted in a party convention or caucus and enunciated by the party's presidential candidate or its congressional leaders. The voters in each state and district choose between these two platforms and elect to office the members of the party whose platform best indicates the direction they feel the country should take. The party winning the presidency and a majority of the seats in Congress is then mandated to implement its platform by passing the requisite legislation and taking the necessary actions in the executive branch. (Presumably with a national platform adhered to by all the party's candidates it is unlikely that each branch will be controlled by different parties). The losing party becomes the loyal opposition and tries to present an alternative set of policies. These should maintain the clear distinction between the two parties, and the next election should be a referendum on the actions of the majority party.[20]

The responsible party model requires completely cohesive and very partisan parties in the Congress to implement this model. Issues and votes are "party votes," with the members of each party voting as a bloc and following the direction of their party leaders. Only in this way will the party positions be clearly drawn so all those voting for one party over another are voting for or against the same nationally uniform alternatives. Within the legislature this requires very tightly organized parties and strong leaders, so that individual members vote the way the leadership desires. Achieving this party unity means limiting the effectiveness of personal and constituency considerations on individual legislators' voting decisions. In the extreme, personal positions should be influential only to the extent that the rest of the party can be persuaded to adopt them. The only decisions that reflect any constituency input are the ones made by the party leaders or the president on the positions and policies deemed necessary to capture the national vote. (It seems likely, however, that if the members of the current Congress had to agree to support the same platform, either the platforms would not resemble the present party platforms or the parties would be quite different.) The major influence individual constituencies have under this system is their choice of a party to represent them in Congress.[21]

The representational models accept a criterion similar to those of the responsible party advocates for evaluating legislative decisions, namely that public policies should reflect the preferences of individual citizens. However, supporters of the representational model argue that a very different process is required to obtain

this reflection accurately. Most proponents of this view start with
the observation on which the intensity and coalition forms of
the representational models is based: that people have both
different preferences on public issues and very different assessments of the relative importance of each issue. The implications
of this statement go beyond saying that victorious electoral
postures may require taking minority stands on some issues, or
that legislators will try to insure the passage of legislation which
is important to their constituents by bargaining with their votes
on unimportant issues. In addition to making this predictive statement about how legislators will behave, proponents of the representational view of how public policy should be made argue that
it is important and necessary for this coalition forming and logrolling to take place. Coalitions are the means a democratic
process has to take into account the feelings of intense minorities
within the electorate.[22] The logrolls also function as compensation
or side-payments to those who feel they will be harmed by the
adoption of a particular policy.[23]

Proponents of this system list several reasons why legislators
must be directly responsive to their constituents' conceptions
of the public interest and to their determinations of what public
policies should be adopted to get the appropriate coalitions and
logrolls.[24] The legislature's function is to choose among different
programs, activities, and agencies and to oversee the administration, delivery, and distribution of these activities by the executive
branch. The specific decisions authorizing, funding, and overseeing
these different programs and agencies, which are legislative decisions, have more impact on the various constituencies and are more
important to them than the broader statements of the party platforms. Consequently, it becomes crucial for legislators to represent
the views of the people of their districts and not the positions of
the party leaders at the time these decisions are made. It is also
more important to have the constituencies represented at this
point than in the party caucuses or conventions, which do not
deal with specific legislative items, because each legislator pre-

sumably knows his district and its concerns better than the national party leaders. Even the behavioral version of the coalition model, in which the parties embody the necessary negotiations and bargains which result in observable party voting, implies that the logrolling should take place at the time the votes are being cast on specific bills and not in party caucuses. The constituencies are then in a position to choose their representatives on the basis of their stands on issues *and* how well they have represented their constituents.

Proponents of the trustee, or statesman, view of legislative behavior believe the legislature's function is to reach a determination of the collective interest on public issues. These public issues involve decisions on complicated and intricate matters which individual citizens are not able to understand and about which they are not able to determine their own particular interests, let alone the interests of the society at large. It is necessary, therefore, to rely upon elected representatives to make the decisions, rather than have direct, referendum-type votes on each issue. Legislators have greater expertise and information which they can bring to bear on questions of public policy and which they can use in arriving at an agreement on the collective interest on these questions. Agreement can best, or possibly only, be reached through well reasoned and measured debate on specific program proposals. Debate will, or should, define and illuminate the "public interest" associated with each proposal; "legislators are always involved in mutual enlightenment and reconciliation of the complex views they represent as a group."[25] Once this enlightenment and reconciliation are accomplished, it should be fairly easy for the legislature to decide whether to accept, reject, or amend a proposal.

For a variety of reasons, legislators have considerable discretion in the positions they adopt and the policies they propose that leaves them free from particular local interests and pressures. For example, Congress should, and does, debate whether the nation needs an expanded airport system, not whether federal funds should be used to expand the airport in a given city. The latter decision should be made after legislation determining that the country needs a new airport system is passed. Legislators are not free from public opinion, to be sure, but are expressing the component of public opinion which can be brought into agreement on national goals and objectives. Maass proposes that the electorate's responsibility is to choose, "men who, in their personal capacity, and in virtue of their character are fitted to discharge the task of deliberation and discussion at the parliamentary stage," and subsequently that, "periodically the elctorate, using this standard (the responsibility of seeking agreement on objectives), will pass formal judgement on the legislators; between these periods the electorate and the community will provide intelligence to the legislators which the latter will evaluate and use as they see fit in the exercise of their discretion."[26]

In addition to having constituents adopt this trusteeship view of the legislator and enforcing it upon individual legislators, there are a variety of ways in which this model can be implemented. One way of course is to have Congress debate only matters of general policy, such as whether to expand the nation's airport system, and not matters of local interest. Legislators will also be freer of these demands if their constituents are not concerned about public issues and do not pay attention to how their representatives vote, which was one of the justifications offered for legislators' adopting this trusteeship role.[27] Finally, the political system can be structured in such a way that representatives' incentives to respond to district demands are reduced. The proposals to lengthen the terms of individual representatives is an example of such a structural change.[28]

AN EMPIRICAL STUDY

Any discussion of how the legislative branch should be structured to make it fit one of these normative models and of what reforms are needed for moving toward the desired system requires information on which influences are currently important and which model the present system most resembles. If the positions of the party leaders explain a high proportion of the votes cast and seem to be more important than constituencies, it implies that Congress is closer to the responsible party model than one of the representational models. In that case, a supporter of the responsible party doctrine who was unhappy with current congressional decisions would want to be careful about making any reforms in the system but might want to consider how to change the parties' geographic bases of support.[29] A believer in the coalition model, however, would want to consider ways to reduce the importance of party leaders and increase the effect of constituency interests. Similarly, if constituency was found to be more important than the party leaders, a responsible party advocate would want to propose reforms to weaken constituency influence and increase that of the party leadership.[30] In any case, systematic empirical evidence on which influences are important in individual legislator's decisions is required for these considerations.

This study provides some of this empirical evidence. The emphasis will be on the roll call voting behavior of United States senators during the years 1961–1963 and the relative influence of constituency and leadership considerations on these votes. The Senate was chosen for study primarily because it used formal roll call votes more frequently than did the House. These yield more information about the voting decisions of each member and about the senate collectively on different pieces of legislation than is available for the House. More information also is available about each of the constituencies, and there are fewer members to be analyzed. The years 1961–1963 were selected to avoid the atypicalness of the period following President Kennedy's assassination and the Johnson-Democratic landslide of 1964, which would make generalizations to other Congresses difficult. Because the study itself was initiated in 1967, the 87th Congress then was the most recent, "typical" period.

[2] A Model of Legislative Voting Behavior

The appropriate way to evaluate the approaches to legislative behavior outlined in Chapter 1 and to estimate the magnitudes of the influences in these explanations is to construct a model explicitly relating senators' votes to the influences contained in each explanation. The idea behind these models is to relate precise measures of senators' positions on different bills to similar measures of the many influences used to explain their positions. The measures can be used to infer statistically which influences are important in determining how different senators voted. If the statistical models are to adequately test the previous approaches to legislative voting and their different variants, they must include specific variables to represent the influences emphasized by the various versions of each explanation.

A FORMAL REPRESENTATION OF SENATE VOTING BEHAVIOR

The Statistical Model

The important variables in the different explanations of legislative voting are senators' constituencies, the formal leaders—the floor leaders and whips, the chairman and ranking minority member of the committee reporting a bill, the president, and various informal leaders—the legislative experts, members of the establishment, and possibly the senior partner if both senators from a state are in the same party. The relationships between these influences, or variables, and a senator's observed votes are expressed in the form of linear equations (Eqs. 2.1 and 2.2). The basic model used to represent Democratic senators' voting behavior is

(2.1) $\text{Vote} = a_0 + a_1 \text{ Constituency} + a_2 \text{ Majority Leader} + a_3 \text{ Majority Whip} + a_4 \text{ President} + a_5 \text{ Committee Chairman} + e,$

and the one for Republicans is

(2.2) $\text{Vote} = b_0 + b_1 \text{ Constituency} + b_2 \text{ Minority Leader} + b_3 \text{ Minority Whip} + b_4 \text{ Ranking Minority Committee Member} + b_5 \text{ Policy Committee Chairman} + b_6 \text{ President} + e.$

Because the Democratic floor leader is also chairman of the Democratic Policy Committee, there is no need to include it separately. The e's indicate that these are statistical models and not exact equations. Senators' measured positions on different bills will deviate from the positions predicted by the systematic part of the model because of nonsystematic influences, possible measurement errors, or an omitted influential variable. The e's represent these deviations.

Three other variables, representing aspects of the specialization and club versions of the organizational model, were added to these basic models for specific senators. A variable similar to the committee chairman variable but representing a predominant liberal or conservative on the reporting committee was the first. These committee member variables were included because they represent specific sources of expertise for many senators. Senators who have conducted hearings on a subject, deliberated the content and potential impact of specific bills, and then signed and defended the committee report or a minority report will be familiar with the issues and natural sources for expert opinion on a bill's merits or demerits. The committee chairmen and minority leaders are the obvious persons to provide this information. This is not likely to be true for most northern Democrats, however. All committee chairmen but one were southerners or southwesterners who took more conservative views of most legislation and represented quite different constituencies than the more liberal northern and eastern Democratic senators. Consequently, liberal senators are likely to rely on their liberal colleagues on the committee reporting the bill, rather than the chairman, for information on how to vote when a bill reaches the floor. A similar process is expected to hold for the more conservative, and generally western, Republicans, who might be considered part of the conservative coalition.[1] The committee liberal variable was included in the models for most nonsouthern Democratic senators, the exceptions being some senators from the southwestern and Rocky Mountain states. The committee conservative variable was added to the models for particularly conservative Republicans.

The second variable added was a senior senator variable. If both senators from a state were in the same party, then the senior senator was included as an explanatory variable in the model for the junior member.[2] Finally, there were also several hypotheses about regional or establishment leaders included in some individual models. The variable representing Senator Russell best exemplifies this. Russell was purportedly the spokesman, strategist, and dean of the southern senators. He also was the clearest example of White's Senate type and a charter member of the inner club. Thus, if the club model is appropriate for roll call voting, Russell should be an important influence on senators' voting behavior, at least among southern Democrats. There were other informal leader variables added on a geographic or personality basis. Some of these additions resulted from statements made by people familiar with the Senate. Others represent estimates by the researcher of which senators played important informational roles.

The variables included in each senator's equation, in addition to the ones shown in Eqs. 2.1 and 2.2 are shown in Table 2.1.

TABLE 2.1. HYPOTHESIZED MODELS FOR EACH SENATOR

Senator	State	Variables added to Equation 2.1
A. Eastern Democrats		
Dodd	Conn.	
Muskie	Maine	Committee liberal
Smith	Mass.	Committee liberal, Muskie, Pastore
Pastore	R.I.	Committee liberal
Pell	R.I.	Senior senator
Williams	N.J.	Committee liberal
Clark	Pa.	Committee liberal
Douglas	Ill.	Committee liberal
Hartke	Ind.	—
Hart	Mich.	Senior senator, committee liberal
McNamara	Mich.	Committee liberal
Lausche	Ohio	—
Young	Ohio	Committee liberal, senior senator
Proxmire	Wisc.	Committee liberal, Douglas
Humphrey	Minn.	Committee liberal
McCarthy	Minn.	Kerr[a]
Symington	Mo.	Committee liberal
Long	Mo.	Senior senator
Burdick	N. Dak.	Committee liberal
Gore	Tenn.	Committee liberal, senior senator
Kefauver	Tenn.	Sparkman
Byrd	W.Va.	Senior senator
Randolph	W.Va.	Committee liberal
B. Southern Democrats		
Byrd	Va.	
Robertson	Va.	Senior senator, Russell
Hill	Ala.	Russell, Sparkman[b]
Sparkman	Ala.	Senior senator, Russell
Fulbright	Ark.	Senior senator, dummy for bills from For. Relations Comm.[c]

TABLE 2.1 (continued)

Senator	State	Variables added to Equation 2.1
McClellan	Ark.	Russell
Holland	Fla.	Russell
Smathers	Fla.	Russell, senior senator
Russell	Ga.	
Talmadge	Ga.	Senior senator
Ellender	La.	Russell
Long	La.	Russell, senior senator
Eastland	Miss.	Russell
Stennis	Miss.	Russell, senior senator
Ervin	N.C.	Russell
Jordan	N.C.	Russell, senior senator, Ellender, Johnston
Johnston	S.C.	Russell
Thurmond	S.C.	Russell, senior senator
C. Western Democrats		
Yarborough	Tex.	Committee liberal, Kefauver
Kerr	Okla.	—
Monroney	Okla.	Senior senator
Hayden	Ariz.	—
Carroll	Colo.	—
Church	Idaho	Committee liberal
Mansfield	Mont.	Mean senator[d]
Metcalf	Mont.	—
Bible	Nev.	—
Cannon	Nev.	Senior senator
Chavez	N.M.	—
Anderson	N.M.	Senior senator
Moss	Utah	—
Hickey	Wyo.	Senior senator
McGee	Wyo.	—
Engle	Calif.	Committee liberal
Morse	Oreg.	Committee liberal
Neuberger	Oreg.	Committee liberal, senior senator
Jackson	Wash.	Senior senator
Magnuson	Wash.	—
Bartlett	Alaska	Committee liberal

Senator	State	Variables added to Equation 2.1
Gruening	Alaska	Committee liberal, Morse[e]
Long	Hawaii	—

Senator	State	Variables added to Equation 2.2

D. Eastern Republicans

Senator	State	Variables added to Equation 2.2
Bush	Conn.	—
Smith	Maine	—
Saltonstall	Mass.	—
Bridges	N.H.	Committee conservative
Murphy	N.H.	Senior senator
Cotton	N.H.	Senior senator, committee conservative
Aiken	Vt.	—
Prouty	Vt.	Senior senator
Boggs	Del.	Senior senator
Williams	Del.	—
Case	N.J.	—
Javits	N.Y.	—
Keating	N.Y.	Senior senator
Scott	Pa.	—
Cooper	Ky.	—
Morton	Ky.	Senior senator
Beall	Md.	Senior senator
Butler	Md.	Committee conservative

E. Midwestern and Western Republicans

Senator	State	Variables added to Equation 2.2
Dirksen	Ill.	Committee conservative, mean Republican[f]
Capehart	Ind.	Committee conservative
Wiley	Wisc.	—
Hickenlooper	Iowa	—
Miller	Iowa	Senior senator
Carlson	Kans.	Senior senator[g]
Pearson	Kans.	Senior senator
Curtis	Nebr.	Senior senator, committee conservative
Hruska	Nebr.	Committee conservative, Curtis[b]
Young	N.Dak.	—

TABLE 2.1 (continued)

Senator	State	Variables added to Equation 2.2
Case	S.Dak.	Senior senator
Mundt	S.Dak.	Committee conservative
Tower	Tex.	Committee conservative
Goldwater	Ariz.	Committee conservative
Allott	Colo.	—
Dworshak	Idaho	Committee conservative
Bennett	Utah	Committee conservative
Kuchel	Calif.	—
Fong	Hawaii	—

[a]Suggested by James Sundquist, The Brookings Institution, in an interview, March 13, 1968.

[b]See discussion on senior senators in Chapter 4.

[c]This variable takes on the value 1 for bills reported by the Foreign Relations Committee, 0 otherwise.

[d]This is the mean Guttman scale score of all senators. The mean scale score of only Democrats was also used.

[e]Suggested by Sam Merrick, Office of the Mayor, Boston, Mass., in an interview in February 1968. Mr. Merrick formerly was Administrative Assistant to Senator Morse.

[f]This is the mean Guttman scale score of all Republicans.

[g]The senior senator was Schoeppel until his death after the 1961 session. Schoeppel was excluded from the analysis because of a lack of observations due to his death and absences in 1961.

The interpretation of these models requires some explanation. The variables included in the senators' equations are the influences expected to have a direct effect on their voting behavior by at least one of the different models. The coefficients in these equations measure how the senators' positions are expected to change with changes in the positions of each influence, independently of changes in the other variables in the equation. For example, the coefficient a_1 in Eq. 2.1 estimates the expected effect on the votes of a Democratic senator of a change in his constituency's position, given that there is no change in the positions of the party leaders, the president, the committee chairman, and any other variables included in the equation. Likewise a_2 is the voting change expected from a change in the position of the majority leader, given that there is no change in the position of the majority whip, the president, the constituency, and so forth.

Statements about holding other leaders constant may appear meaningless, or possibly misleading, since in another equation the whip's positions are predicted to change if the majority leader's position changes. This does not invalidate the previous equations or interpretations, however. As long as it is possible for each explanatory variable in the equation to behave independently of the others, then it is possible to discuss and estimate the direct effect of each explanatory variable on a senator's voting behavior independently of the other influences. The various equations clearly indicate that this independent behavior is possible. For example, the majority leader is not the sole determinant, let alone a perfect predictor, of the whip's positions, which are also affected by the whip's constituency and various nonsystematic effects. Because of these other effects it is possible to have changes in the whip's votes unaccompanied by changes in the majority leader's votes. If there is sufficient uncorrelated variation in these two senators' positions, even though one may exert an influence on the other, it is possible to estimate the direct effect each leader has on the other senators.

The estimated coefficients in Eqs. 2.1 and 2.2 do not provide estimates of the total effect on senators' voting behavior resulting from changes in one of the explanatory variables. For example, in the previous illustration, a_2 was the direct effect on a Democratic senator's position expected from a change in the majority leader's position. The total effect expected to result from the change in the majority leader's position is this direct effect, *plus* a_3 times the change in the majority whip's position resulting from this change in the leader's position. This estimate of the change in the whip's position must come from the estimated effect of the leader on the whip obtained by estimating the appropriate equation for the whip. The implications of this discussion of the direct and total effects associated with the various explanatory variables apply to many of the variables included in these equations. Other examples would be the constituency and senior senator and the president and party leader variables.

The various explanations of legislative behavior discussed in Chapter 1 are all presented in terms of which influences have direct effects on senators' voting behavior. The cue source version of the organizational model for example maintains that senators' votes will be determined by the positions of the senators from whom they take cues, even though these cues are possibly being used to proxy constituency positions. In these cases, the cue sources and not the constituencies are the direct determinants of senators' voting behavior. Conversely, according to any of the representational models, constituencies have a direct effect on legislators' votes even though senators may be consulting with colleagues to learn how certain legislation may effect their constituents. In these cases, the constituency variables have a direct influence. In both examples senators are attempting to vote with their constituents, but the direct influences on their votes are different. In the former case, votes are cast by adopting the positions of various cue sources, while in the latter case, the votes are the legislators' own assessments of their constituencies' positions. These two different models are predicting that different variables will directly influence senators' votes. It is important to obtain as accurate estimates of these direct influences as possible if the results are to be helpful in evaluating the different explanations of legislative behavior.

One of the most crucial considerations in getting accurate estimates of the effects of each influence is making sure that there are no systematic influences of senators' voting behavior excluded from the equations. There are excluded influences, of course, as indicated by the e's in Eqs. 2.1 and 2.2, but they must not be correlated with the included variables. The effect of excluding a systematic influence that is correlated with one of the variables from the equation is inaccurate, or biased, estimates of the influence of the variables included in the equation, and the magnitude of this bias is related to the amount of correlation between the included and excluded variables. If any of the variables associated with one of the explanations are excluded from the equations, and if this explanation happens to be valid, then the estimates of the influence of the variables in the equation, and thereby of the included explanations, will be inaccurate. The result of this inaccuracy will be erroneous conclusions about the importance of the included explanations. The only way to overcome this problem is to make sure that all systematic influences on legislators' behavior are included in the estimated equation. This, of course, is why the variables associated with each explanation of legislative voting are included in one equation and why a multivariate statistical procedure is required.

EXPLANATIONS OF LEGISLATIVE VOTING AND THE STATISTICAL MODELS

In a well designed study there are usually several variables uniquely associated with each alternative explanation. The different explanations are evaluated on the basis of how statistically significant its variables are and on the strength of their influence on the dependent variable. If all or most of the variables associated with one approach are not statistically different from zero, it is possible to reject that approach in favor of one or more of the alternatives. This will be difficult in the case of Senate voting because for most of the variables a significant coefficient is consistent with several different ways of viewing the Senate. However it may still be possible to suggest ways of discriminating among the different models, or at least to suggest the relative importance of each. This can be done by examining the distribution of the magnitudes of the coefficients among the senators, their stability under different circumstances and the overall fit of these equations both to individual senators and to different types of legislation. For example, both the organizational approach and the behavioral

version of the coalition representational model predict that the
formal party leaders will be influential in the voting behavior of
the individual rank-and-file members. The leadership model
argues this because of the leaders' ability to manipulate such
resources as committee assignments, access to the president, and
control of the scheduling of legislation to obtain the support of
other senators. The behavioral coalition model's justification is
that the party leaders are the organizers of and focal points for
the various bargains and vote trades constituting the coalitions
which form the legislative parties. However, the organizational
model, at least implicitly, excludes the influence of constituencies,[3] while the representational coalition concept of the legislature argues that on different issues, constituency preferences
and their intensity strongly influence the trades senators can
make, which coalitions they will join, and their actual votes on
certain issues. According to the organizational approach the
coefficients on the constituency variables will be zero, or at least
very small, while the representational model predicts that these
same coefficients will be positive and statistically significant but
not account for all of a senator's systematic voting behavior.
Even if the coefficients on the formal leader variables are significant, it is still possible to discriminate between the two approaches
by examining the size of the constituency coefficients. In this
manner the relative sizes and significances of the estimated coefficients in each senator's equation can be used to further discriminate among the approaches outlined in Chapter 1 and their
different variations. These implications of the various models
and the results which would support each one must be outlined
prior to the analysis, however.

The Organizational Model

In the most straightforward version of the traditional organizational model, the voting of each senator is determined by the
positions of the formal party leaders. These formal leaders, in
order of hypothesized importance, are the party floor leaders, the

whips, the chairman and ranking minority member of the committee reporting the bill being considered, and the chairman of the
Policy Committee for Republicans. The expected role of the
president in this model is not clearly spelled out. Truman spends
a considerable amount of space discussing the relationship between
the president and the party leaders, particularly the presidential
party's leader.[4] He seems to conclude during this discussion that
most of the presidential influence is exerted through the party
leader and not directly from the president to individual legislators.
This conclusion would be supported if the coefficients on the
presidential variable were consistently close to and not statistically
different from zero. This model, then, predicts that most senators
will have large and statistically significant coefficients for the
formal leadership variables, with the coefficients for the party
leaders being the largest and most frequently significant of the
leadership effects.

The traditional organizational model further hypothesizes that
constituencies are not systematically important and thus should
have zero coefficients in most models. Likewise, there should be
little role for informal leaders, such as specialists or regional
spokesmen, and so the informal leaders included in the models and
the committee liberal and committee conservative variables should
also have zero or insignificant coefficients. Finally, the organizational models seem to imply that on "must" legislation, as defined
by the party leaders, the leadership will try to apply extra pressure
and thus be able to obtain the desired support for the bill. If this
model is appropriate for most senators, not only should the coefficients on the formal leaders be large, but the models should
provide a better fit on those bills defined as "must legislation."
These models should also provide the weakest explanation for
voting on bills where the leadership is indifferent.

The club or establishment version of the organizational model
predicts that specific seniority leaders will have a consistent
influence on senators' voting behavior. Presumably these influences will be in addition to the influences of the formal party

leaders who are also part of the establishment. These seniority leaders should be influential at least on a regional basis and among other members of the club if this version of the organizational model is useful for predicting legislative behavior on a systematic basis. For example, this approach would predict that Senator Russell would be important in the voting behavior of southern, and possibly southwestern and Rocky Mountain, Democrats, since he is usually listed as one of the establishment's charter members.

The specialization and cue source version of the organizational model is similar in some respects to the formal leadership version discussed above. The party leaders and whips, with their knowledge of the legislation and high visibility, are natural sources for cues on how to vote. The chairman and ranking minority member of the reporting committee also play important roles in this explanation. At the same time, the committee liberal and committee conservative variables should be important influences in this model. It was Matthews and Stimpson's inclusion of similar variables for the House, although they were not tied to the committees, which set their simulation apart from previous organizational studies.[5] The argument for including these variables was that with the complexity of most legislation and the high degree of specialization, senators must rely on the opinions and positions of specialists in each legislative area for information on how to vote. The most knowledgeable individuals in any area should be the senators on the committee which held hearings and researched each bill. Thus, the committee variables, and particularly the ideological ones, should be important in many senators' models if the information source model is appropriate. These variables are not included in the formal leadership version of the organizational model, which leads to a way to discriminate between the two.

The cue source conception of how senators vote also makes the strongest argument for the importance of the senior senator variable. This should be especially true for freshmen and other fairly new senators. For junior senators, one of the clearest and

best sources of information about how to vote and how to function in general will be the senator's senior colleague. Senior
senators usually have been around, know the way business is
conducted and what is being said by the various participants, and
probably have been reelected at least once themselves. Thus, it
would seem natural that recent arrivals in the senate would look
to them for advice and counseling. These influences will probably
decline as the junior senators gain both experience and their own
information sources. It is these nonformal leader influences, the
committee liberal and conservative and the senior senator variables,
which will serve to distinguish the cue source version of the organizational model from the traditional formal leadership version
that confines itself to the party and seniority leaders. All these
organizational models predict that constituency does not have a
direct and consistent effect on senators' voting behavior.

The Representational Model

The simplest of the representational models was the majoritarian version. In this version, representatives are assumed to be
voting as a majority of the people in their districts would if the
procedures were available for them to do so. This seems to be the
notion behind the Miller and Stokes examination of constituency
influence on Congress.[6] Their constituency variable was simply
the mean opinion score of the people sampled in each district on
the issues of social welfare, foreign involvement, and civil rights,
without regard to how strongly different people felt about each
of the three issues. If congressmen were responding to the Miller
and Stokes estimate of the average opinion in their districts, it
would seem to imply the majoritarian version. The intensity or
saliency version of the representational model varies from the
majoritarian version only so far as it predicts that the positions
taken by legislators wanting to improve their chances of reelection
are ones which recognize the existence of intense minorities
within their constituencies. Representatives' votes, then, will not
correspond to the mean of constituents' opinions but will accom-

modate these minority feelings. Unfortunately, the model being developed here will not be able to distinguish between the majoritarian and the intensity versions. However, both these versions predict that the only consistent influence on senators' voting behavior will be the positions of their constituents.

A representational model expounded by MacRae gives the same results for the estimated coefficients but then goes on to suggest which bills will be explained better by this explanation.[7] In MacRae's model, congressmen make compromises between their own preferences and those of their constituents. The more important an issue is to district residents, and hence the larger the impact of the congressmen's votes on their chances for reelection, the more likely the compromises are to favor the constituents' positions. For example, in many districts, civil rights votes or votes on bills with strong local economic impacts are more likely to reflect constituency positions than votes on foreign affairs. According to the MacRae model, constituency should be the only important variable in senators' voting equations, and these constituency models should do a better job of explaining senators' votes on issues which are important to their constituents. Miller and Stokes's results were consistent with this prediction. They found that the correlation between their majoritarian constituency variables and congressmen's votes was highest on civil rights bills, lowest on foreign involvement issues, with social welfare legislation falling in between.[8] The MacRae model also predicts that the constituency influence will be higher for senators from states with closely contested elections, where a wrong vote could lead to possible defeat,[9] and for senators who are nearing the end of their terms and must campaign for reelection.

The final constituency-only model was the coalition version. This version predicts that representatives will vote with their constituents' positions, but it includes the possibility of legislators trading for other members' support on the issues important to them. A model of this process must be able to predict which coalitions will form, on what issues votes will be exchanged, and by which senators. Constructing such a model is a difficult task.[10] The implications of this coalition version for the equations to be estimated here differ from the other representational models in one respect. Constituency should still be the only important consistent determinant of senators' votes, and, as with the MacRae model, the constituency models should predict voting behavior well where bills are important to senators' constituencies and poorly for unimportant bills. However, on bills where the constituency variable predicts well the votes of senators in groups A and B, whose constituents had opposing preferences on the bills but agreed that the bills were very important, it will predict poorly for senators in group C, whose constituents felt there were other bills which were more important. These group C senators then are voting with the members of either A or B in exchange for the latters' support on the bills which are important to group C's constituents. It should be possible to check the votes cast by the members of group C on their poorly fit bills to see if they were supporting the positions of the members of either A or B, and if the members of A and B were reciprocating on the bills which were fit well for members of group C and poorly fit for themselves. For example, Rocky Mountain senators might vote with their states on public power, mining, ranching, and development bills, which are important to their constituents, and vote with southern senators on civil rights or eastern senators on urban bills. The southerners and easterners, on the other hand, will be voting with their constituents on these latter bills but with the western senators on the power and development bills.[11] This would lead to the result that western senators' votes on civil rights and on urban bills would be predicted poorly, as would the votes of southerners and easterners on the power and development bills, while there would be good fits for the votes of westerners on the latter bills and the southerners and easterners on the former bills.

The Behavioral Version of the Coalition Model

The final model to be considered is a behavioral version of the coalition representational model. The most distinguishing feature of this model is that it is a hybrid of some or all of the variations of the organization and representation explanations. This is hardly surprising, since it is an attempt to "explain" some of the organizationalists observations about legislative behavior with a sophisticated representational scheme. One of the reasons suggested in Chapter 1 for parties and other internal organizations was that the negotiating and bargaining implied by the coalition model requires too much of the legislators time and resources. Thus, the party leaders and whips function as clearinghouses for information about what bills are important to which senators and what these senators are willing to sacrifice to get their important bills passed. The leaders are brokers in the sense that they then arrange these trades and are also responsible for seeing that trades and bargains are kept. If they are successful, then all the individual senators have to do is agree to vote with the party leaders on most bills in exchange for the leaders' assurances of support for their important bills. Consequently, the members of the party coalitions will have significant coefficients for the floor leaders or whips.

This behavioral coalition model also hypothesizes that the Democratic leaders were likely to be stronger than the Republican leaders. The centralized leadership in the Democratic party gives the leaders more resources to use in arranging and enforcing the bargains worked out by the leaders. Senators who will not go along with the trades will find themselves unable to get good committee assignments or desirable office space. They also will not be able to obtain consideration for their "important" bills. The authority to control the scheduling of legislation, which rests with the majority leader, who was a Democrat in this case, is also a useful tool in arranging and maintaining these voting agreements. The leader can try to bring up the bills on which he has worked out a series of trades fairly close together so that there is less chance of the agreements being broken. During the session of Congress being studied here, the Democratic leader could also use the resources of the president to obtain votes and to enforce agreements.

It is also quite likely that less formally organized coalitions existed either within or between members of the two parties. Groups of senators may have gotten together and worked out trades and agreements about certain bills independently of the party positions. The committee liberal and committee conservative variables could be representing these groups just as easily as they are representing legislative experts who provide informational cues to other members of the Senate. The liberal or conservative on the reporting committee then is merely the focal point or organizer for the efforts of these smaller coalitions. Members of the reporting committee are chosen because they are in positions to influence the content of the bills reported from the com- mittees as well as being the most knowledgeable in their content and effects. This familiarity with the bills then places the com- mittee members at an advantage in deciding what trades and compromises can be made to obtain passage for the bill. This hypothesis is not inconsistent with the organizational arguments for the importance of these informal leader variables which was based on the committee members' expertise and specialization. However, the coalition model is arguing that their influence is derived from considerations related to coalition building and the relationship of the bill to various constituencies as well as to their familiarity with the technical content of the bill.

It is the expected influence both of the formal and informal leadership variables and of the constituency variables which sets the behavioral coalition model apart from the organizational and the representational models mentioned previously. This hybrid model, which is in part a representational explanation, still retains the idea that senators will vote as their constituents wish on the bills which are important to them and only deviate from their constituency on bills where the constituency is completely indif- ferent. Thus, the coefficients on the constituency variables should be significant, but not as large or as able to explain as high a proportion of the votes as if the pure representational model were more appropriate. As with the other representational models, senators from states with close elections are likely to have larger constituency coefficients, as are senators coming up for reelection.

Finally, the behavioral coalition version suggests that bills which are important in many constituencies, such as civil rights, should have better fits than those bills which are unimportant. Similarly, on any one particular bill, the models should have better fits for those senators whose constituencies are most concerned about the bill, just as for the coalition model.

The Trusteeship Explanation

With the exception of Matthews and Stimpson's ideological version of the trusteeship explanation, the trusteeship approach is characterized by the absence of any systematic influences on senators' voting behavior. Votes are cast on the basis of the individual members' determinations of the public interest and their assessment of each bill's relationship to this interest, which is gained through extended debate and deliberation. These influences are all unmeasured by the statistical models presented in this chapter. Support for the trusteeship model, then, would be indicated if these statistical models could not explain senators' voting behavior. Significant constituency coefficients, unaccompanied by significant coefficients on any of the other variables, could also indicate the existence of the trusteeship model. Miller and Stokes have argued that part of the correlation between constituency opinion and congressional voting can be accounted for by the fact that congressmen vote their own opinions and that their opinions are correlated with their constituents' opinions.[12] Since separate variables for senators' opinions and their perceptions of constituency opinions are not included in these models, there is no way to ascertain if this process is accounting for any observed constituency influence. If this is the appropriate explanation for any important constituency effects, then there should be little

variation in the ability of the constituency variable to predict
voting behavior among groups of senators and types of legislation.
At the same time, constituency effects should be invariant with
the competitiveness of the district or the amount of time before a
senator must seek reelection. If senators are voting their own
preferences and are not directly influenced by their constituents,
then the only constituency input to legislative decisions comes
through the recruitment and selection of senators.

The discussion of the evidence needed to support the trusteeship
model finishes the presentation of the various approaches to
explaining legislative behavior and the empirical results needed to
support each approach. It is useful to keep in mind that this is a
statistical study in which the importance of different influences
will be inferred from the relationships observed between individual
senators' votes and the positions of the different influence sources.
The models can be evaluated on the basis of which influences are
most important and on their ability to explain the votes cast by
different senators on specific bills.

[3] Measuring Senate Voting Behavior

LEGISLATIVE PREFERENCES

The key to estimating the relationships between senators' voting behavior and the various influences on it is the development of clear and unambiguous measures for the variables shown in Eqs. 2.1 and 2.2 and in Table 2.1. Ideally such measures would provide a precise assessment of each senator's position on each bill and a similar assessment of the positions of each influence. It would then be a relatively simple matter to relate senators' positions to the positions of the different influences. Unfortunately, easily obtainable measures do not exist, and considerable care and thought must go into the development and evaluation of statistically useful variables.

The Senators

The first obstacle is simply getting a measure of each senator's position on the different bills being considered. Many bills do not provide continuous, observable, and readily quantifiable measures of their contents. Even where such measures may exist conceptually, such as where to set the minimum wage, there are no procedures currently available for getting senators to reveal their positions. The best devices available for getting public disclosure of senators' positions on different issues are the roll call votes used to amend and pass bills. Senators must vote yes or no if they vote on these roll calls, thus revealing their positions on specific questions. Various legislative scholars have shown that simple Guttman scale analysis can be used to order these votes from strongest to weakest support for a bill and have used the resulting scale to rank senators' positions.[1] This provides at least an ordinal measure of each senator's position on each bill. This is the technique which will be used here, even though it creates some potential problems for the statistical analysis, which will be discussed subsequently and in Appendix B.

Guttman scaling was originally developed as a means of analyzing sets of questions in attitudinal surveys.[2] It rests on the assumption that the responses to a set of questions corresponding to different points on a single attitudinal dimension held by the respondents will exhibit specific ordered and cumulative properties. These properties are that all people agreeing with a particular statement, that schools should be integrated, for example, will also agree with all milder statements, such as that transportation and public accommodations should not be segregated. Similarly, people who disagree with the statement that schools should be integrated will also disagree with stronger statements, such as that neighborhoods and private clubs should be integrated. A set of questions exhibiting this characteristic is said to constitute a scale (in this example an integration scale), and respondents can be grouped and ranked according to the questions with which they agreed and disagreed. In a perfect scale, it is possible to know an individual's responses to each question simply by knowing in which group the person is placed or the person's rank score. Empirically, the Guttman procedure orders the questions to minimize the number of nonscale responses. It then assigns respondents to a group, depending on which questions they agreed and disagreed.

In legislative roll call analysis, the votes on amendments to a bill and the vote for passage of the bill are used as the "questions," and these are ordered from least to most support for the bill in accordance with the observed pattern of votes. This process is illustrated in Figure 3.1. The horizontal axis in this diagram measures the underlying dimension of the scale, the level of the minimum wage, the dollars appropriated, and so on, and the vertical axis represents the proportion of senators taking a given position. (A continuous function rather than the more appropriate discrete form is shown for the sake of convenience.) The votes on the bill and the different amendments to it are shown as points on the horizontal axis. These points represent the "location" of each vote on the underlying scale and are labeled a_1, a_2, a_3, and a_4. Application of the Guttman scale method, then, would suggest that each senator will vote for any amendment located to the left of his position and against any proposal to the right. (Right and left refer only to directions in the diagram.) All senators located to the left of a_1, then, vote negatively on all votes. They are subsequently scored a zero. All senators located between a_1 and a_2 presumably vote affirmatively on the proposal labelled a_1 and negatively on all others. These senators are given a score of one, and so forth. The senators to the right of a_4 vote affirmatively on all votes, and in this case, with four votes in the scale, are scored fours.

An example of a set of votes which scaled perfectly was the effort to extend the life of the Civil Rights Commission in 1961.

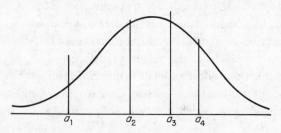

FIGURE 3.1.

The horizontal axis in this case is the length of extension. Proposed extensions were being added to a State-Justice-Judiciary Appropriations Bill. The first vote was an attempt to prevent consideration of this addition to the appropriations bill. This would have effectively terminated the commission—an extension of zero years—and corresponds to vote a_1 in Figure 3.1. The next vote was on a proposal to make the commission a permanent agency and corresponds to a_4. This vote was followed by votes on a four-year extension, a_3, and then a two-year extension, a_2. All senators *favoring the four-year extension also favored a two-year extension, and those opposing the two-year extension opposed both a four-year and permanent extension. Individual senators were scored from four to zero depending upon which amendments they supported and which ones they opposed.

Guttman scales were constructed for each of 36 issues in the 87th Congress (1961–1962), 18 from each session, and 25 issues in 1963. In 52 cases, the votes comprising each scale were limited to the amendments on a single bill, so that in only 9 cases do the scales include roll call votes taken on several separate bills. In most of these 9 cases, the votes clearly relate to a single issue, such as impacted school aid, or the national debt limit.[3] (For convenience, however, all 61 issues are referred to as bills.) The Guttman scales, the amendments used to construct them, and summary statistics are shown in Appendix 3.1, at the end of this chapter. With only a few amendments available on each bill, the range, and thus the number, of categories of each scale is limited.[4] This limitation should be offset by the advantage of having a clearer idea of what the scales are measuring, for example, senators' positions on the Area Redevelopment Act.

The votes used to construct the scales comprise 46 percent, 36 percent, and 54 percent of all the roll call votes in 1961, 1962, and 1963, respectively. However, many of the excluded roll calls duplicated the ones in the scales because the same senators were voting yes or no on both roll calls. This was particularly true in 1962, with the liberals' filibuster over Comsat where votes were taken primarily to consume time. Inclusion of these votes would not increase the information in the scales.

Roll call votes, of course, are not the only decisions made by senators. Legislative decisions are made by voice votes taken during floor consideration and also by committee decisions. However, the Senate does influence the final form of a bill and write legislation with roll call votes, so that understanding how floor votes are cast does provide some insight into the importance of various determinants of public policy. Due to their visibility, one must be cautious in extrapolating from conclusions about roll call voting to conclusions about the determinants of legislative decision making. It may be possible to extrapolate, but it would require additional empirical evidence about the similarities in these decisions.

The Guttman scale scores are measures of the positions of each senator on the different bills. As such, they are the dependent variables to be explained in the process of assessing the importance of the different influences on senators' voting behavior. The scale scores are also measures of positions of the internal influences—the party leaders, the committee chairmen and ranking minority leaders, the committee liberals and conservatives, the senior senators, and the informal and regional leaders. The positions of these internal leaders are represented by the value of the appropriate scale score. For example, the positions of the party leaders are simply the scale scores of Mansfield and Dirksen. The four committee variables were obtained from the scale scores of the appropriate person on the committee reporting each bill, such as the chairman or the most notable conservative member of the committee.

The President

The Guttman scales leave unmeasured the two external influences in the models—the president and the constituencies. It was possible to use the scales to construct a measure of the president's announced position on most bills. The *Congressional*

Quarterly in its yearly *Almanac* reports if the president
favored, opposed, or took no position on each roll call vote.
These assessments are based on the *Congressional Quarterly's*
interpretation of presidential messages, speeches, conferences,
and other public statements.[5] The presidential variable was
constructed by comparing his positions as reported by *CQ* with
the previously and independently constructed senatorial Guttman
scales. When the president was reported as not taking a position
on a vote, it was treated as the opposite of a favorable vote for
scaling purposes. For example, the president was scored as a three
on a five-vote scale if the *CQ* had him taking the liberal position
on the three most conservative votes and taking no position on the
other two. If *CQ* reported the president taking the conservative
position or no position on all five votes, his position was then
scored as zero. This scaling method was facilitated because the
only patterns exhibited in the *CQ* reporting were combinations of
favorable and unfavorable stands, favorable stands and no position,
all favorable, or all unfavorable. There were no combinations of
all three, or no position and unfavorable.

The president's positions scaled almost perfectly. Of the 288
roll calls used to construct the scales, the president was unscalable
on only four of these votes. On an additional 24 he was reported
as taking no position where the scales indicate he should have.
For example, if there were five votes in a scale and the president
was reported supporting the legislation on the first and the third
votes and taking no position on the second, this was counted as
one of the 24 errors. Even counting these no-position errors,
92 percent of the president's positions fit the scales. This percentage rises to 99 if only the erroneous positions are counted
as errors.[6]

The president's position on each bill was assessed by two
variables constructed from his scale scores, a position variable
and a dummy variable for whether or not he had taken a public
position on the bill. The presidential position variable is simply
the president's score on each bill's scale, which places the presi-

dent's announced position on each bill on a scale comparable to the one measuring senators' positions. The presidential dummy variable is a variable scored as one if it appeared to *CQ* that the president had not taken a public position on any of the votes used to construct a scale and zero if he had. This occurred on three bills in 1961 and 1962 and on five bills in 1963.

The dummy variable is required because a value of zero for the presidential position variable indicates either of two quite different presidential positions, and the votes of senators directly influenced by the president will be affected differently in each case. If the president opposed all liberal and supported all conservative amendments to a particular bill, then his scale position would legitimately be scored as zero for that bill. However, if *CQ* indicated that the president had not taken a position on any of these votes, his scale position would also be recorded as zero on the presidential position variable. These two situations provide senators with very different cues about the president's position, though. In the first case, senators who gave considerable weight to the president's positions would be likely to take a conservative position on the bill. In the second case, when there are no announced positions, it is unlikely that these senators will vote as conservatively as they would when the president had opposed all possible positions. The dummy variable will permit senators' votes to show a different response to presidential influence in the two different cases where the presidential position variable is zero.

ESTIMATING CONSTITUENCY POSITIONS

Constructing the ideal constituency variable would require a ranking of each state's population on the scales used to measure the senators' positions on each bill, information on the relative importance people with each scale score attached to each issue, and an estimate of each person's probability of voting. This information would permit the construction of a variable which parallels the constituency variable in the representational model. In this model, congressmen respond to the distribution of opinion among their voting constituents, with more weight given to the preferences of the people most concerned with the issue. The appropriate aggregate constituency preference variable should be the sum of the individual constituents' scale scores weighted by each person's assessment of the importance of each issue and their probability of voting. Obtaining such a measure of constituents' opinion related to the Guttman scales is clearly impossible. It is not even possible to find a public opinion survey question related to most of these bills. Consequently, it was necessary to find an alternative way of estimating what each of the constituencies' positions were on the various bills without the benefit of survey data.

The method used to estimate the constituency variables relies on the relationship between senators' voting behavior and the demographic and regional characteristics of their constituencies. The procedure is based on the assumption that the positions which best reflect both the individual preferences in each state on a bill and the bill's relative importance to different people is correlated with states' demographic and regional characteristics. This means that senators from states within the same region and with equal proportions of farmers, blue-collar workers, urban dwellers, and so forth, will take similar positions on each bill if both are trying to increase their chances for reelection. Another way of putting this assumption is to say that the distribution of preferences on different issues and the relative importance of each issue varies more between different social and economic groups than it does within each group. If this is empirically true, it means that most of the observed variation in political opinion at the state level is accounted for by the mix of social and economic groups in each state's population, at least within fairly broad regions. The distributions of these groups within each state's population can then be used to estimate constituency opinion on each bill for each state. A similar assumption has been used in several previous studies of the effects of constituency on voting behavior.[7] Part of the discussion in Appendix A illustrates this assumption and

shows that it applies to constituency attitudes and senate voting
on the Family Assistance Plan. In the Family Assistance Plan
case, individual attitudes towards the plan, as measured in a survey,
were highly correlated with specific social and economic characteristics, such as race, income, and place of residence.

The social and demographic characteristics describing each state
and used to estimate constituency positions are shown in Table 3.1.
These particular variables were chosen primarily because of their
availability. They were defined on the basis of the characteristics
of each state's voting population as often as possible. All but one
of the demographic variables were measured as a percent of the
population over age twenty-five, as a percent of the labor force, or
as a percent of the families in the state, rather than on a per capita
basis. In addition, except for metropolitanization, the variables
for the southern states were based only on the white population.
This reflects the fact that blacks were systematically excluded from
these voting populations, so that southern senators had no incen-
tive to be responsive to blacks' positions.[8] Since blacks' positions
were likely to be quite different from whites' positions on many
bills, inclusion of the black population in the demographic variables
could lead to erroneous estimates of the *voting* constituency's
positions in southern states.

The assumption is that these demographic variables are highly
correlated with the positions within each constituency that
improved or maintained senators' chances for reelection, even
though these variables were not necessarily the actual determinants of these positions. For example, labor union membership
may have been important in determining how people felt about
specific bills, but union membership data was not readily available
on a state basis and consequently was not included. However,
the variables which were included, such as the occupation mix,
the income data, and the urbanness of each state, should be
sufficiently correlated with union membership to proxy its
effects. This problem with excluded demographic variables means
that the observed relationships between these variables and senators' positions cannot be given any causal interpretation.

TABLE 3.1. VARIABLES USED IN ESTIMATING CONSTITUENCY MODEL

Var. No.	Description
1.[a]	Border states: Delaware, Maryland, West Virginia, Kentucky, Tennessee.
2.	Midwestern states: Ohio, Indiana, Illinois, Michigan, Wisconsin, Minnesota, North Dakota, South Dakota, Iowa, Kansas, Nebraska, Missouri.
3.	Southern states: Virginia, North Carolina, South Carolina, Georgia, Florida, Alabama, Mississippi, Arkansas, Louisiana.
4.	Southwestern states: Oklahoma, Texas, New Mexico, Arizona, Nevada.
5.	Mountain and Far West states: Montana, Idaho, Utah, Colorado, Washington, Oregon, California, Alaska, Hawaii.
6.[b]	Percentage living in metropolitan areas. Metropolitan is defined as cities over 100,000 population and their suburbs.
7.	Percentage of the population over 25 who have completed 12 years or more of schooling, but have not finished college.
8.	Percentage of the population over 25 who have completed college.
9.	Percentage of the employed male labor force employed as farmers and farm managers.
10.	Percentage of the employed male labor force employed as managers, officials, and proprietors, excluding farm.
11.	Percentage of the employed male labor force employed as clerical, sales, or service (except private household) workers.
12.	Percentage of the employed male labor force employed as craftsmen, foreman, operatives, and laborers (except farm and mine).
13.	Percentage of the families and unrelated individuals with incomes between $10,000 and $15,000.
14.	Percentage of the families and unrelated individuals with incomes over $15,000.
15.	Percentage of the over 25 population who are 55 or older.
16.	Farm Bureau membership per 1000 people over 25.
17.	Farm Union membership per 100 people over 25.
18.	Unemployed as a percentage of the civilian labor force.

Sources. Variables 6–15 and 18 are from the 1960 Census of Population. Variables 16 and 17 are from Don F. Hadwiger and Ross B. Talbot, *Pressures and Protests* (San Francisco: Chandler Publishing Co., 1965), pp. 266–267.

[a]Variables 1–5 are expressed as dummies.

[b]The variables for the southern states are only for the white population with the exception of variable 6, which includes the total population.

The estimates of each constituency's position on a given bill was obtained by regressing each senator's scale score on that bill against the set of demographic variables.[9] The outputs of this regression were predicted scale scores for all senators based on the values of the demographic variables for their states. The predicted scale scores were used as the estimates of the constituencies' positions on the bill. Separate regressions were run for each of the bills. This yields predicted values for each senator on each bill. The constituency variables used to estimate the senators' equations were the scale scores on each bill predicted for each senator on the basis of the state's demographic characteristics.[10]

This procedure for estimating constituency positions has its difficulties. One is that it is hard to visualize. The discussion of the Family Assistance Plan legislation in Appendix A gives a detailed illustration of how these constituency variables were derived. A constituency variable for FAP is calculated by the process described here and compared to the constituency variable obtained from the survey data discussed previously. Besides showing that these two constituency variables were highly correlated, this discussion will give a better picture of how the constituency variables described here were obtained.

A greater difficulty, however, is that the procedure used to derive the constituency variables may influence the estimates of the coefficients in the individual senators' equations. The second part of Appendix A gives a formal derivation of the procedures used to obtain these constituency positions and to estimate the influence of the different variables in the senators' equations. These procedures are also simulated for a very simple legislature to explore some of the difficulties pointed out by the formal derivation. The implications both of the formal model and from the simulation are that constituency influence may be overstated and the leaders' influences may be understated. However, the simulation also suggested that there was a high correlation between the actual and the estimated influence of both variables. It is important to be aware of this problem when drawing conclusions from these results.

ESTIMATING SENATORS' VOTING BEHAVIOR

Senators' voting equations, as shown in Eqs. 2.1 and 2.2 and
Table 2.1, were estimated by regressing their Guttman scale scores
on each of the 36 bills from 1961–1962 against the constituency
variables, the two presidential variables, and the Guttman scale
scores of the other senators or variables based on individual
senators in the hypothesized equations. Ordinary regression
analysis was used to estimate the influence on these variables on
senators' votes and to test hypotheses about which influences
might be unimportant. This technique presents several potential
problems given the available data and the models being estimated.
The fact that the dependent variable in each equation, as well
as most of the explanatory variables, are ordinal, Guttman scale
scores constitutes a departure from the traditional uses of the
linear regression model, which usually assume interval data. Using
ordinal data means that some of the assumptions required to
obtain the statistical properties of the estimated coefficients may
be violated. A discussion of these assumptions, how they are
violated and with what possible consequences, is presented in
Appendix B. Each senator's voting equation was subsequently
estimated with a more elaborate statistical procedure which
seemed better suited to the Guttman data. The results using this
alternative statistical technique are also presented in Appendix B.
These results, and the conclusions about senators' voting behavior,
hardly differed from the results using linear regression analysis.
Consequently, it seemed appropriate to present the results using
the simpler procedure.

A second difficulty posed by the use of the Guttman variables
is the interpretation given to the estimated coefficients in each
senator's equation. In cases where there is an interval dependent
variable, it is possible to talk about a given change in one of the
explanatory variables being associated with a particular expected
change in the dependent variable. The magnitude of the expected
change is determined by the size of the estimated coefficient.
This interpretation of the coefficients is more difficult when the
dependent variable is a Guttman scale. For example, it is hard to

say that because of a change in Mansfield's position, another senator's position changed by 0.53 units on a Guttman scale. The best way to interpret the estimated coefficients is on a comparative basis. If Mansfield's coefficient in a second senator's equation is 1.00, it seems reasonably safe to conclude that Mansfield exerted more influence on this second senator's voting than he did on that of the first. Similarly, within any one senator's equation, coefficients of 0.9 on the constituency variable and 0.4 on Dirksen's variable imply that this senator was influenced more by his constituency than by the minority leader.[11]

The final problem with using ordinary regression lies within the models themselves. One of the assumptions of ordinary regression is that the dependent variable in the equation being estimated does not exert any influence on the explanatory variables. In other words, these explanatory variables are independent of the variable being explained. If such influence is present, the two variables have a simultaneous influence on each other, and the estimated coefficients on the explanatory variable will not be the most accurate predictions of its true influence. In these cases a more elaborate estimation procedure, developed for such simultaneous equations was required.

There are several places where such joint influence may be present. The equations for both party leaders contain a variable to represent the mean positions of all senators or of groups of senators. These models incorporate a simultaneous relationship because each leader is expected to influence the voting behavior of the individual senators' who make up these mean position variables. Thus, the mean Republican, mean Democratic, and mean Senate variables are reflecting Dirksen's and Mansfield's behavior as well as exerting their own influence on the two leaders. There is also the possibility that some of the state pairs, if they are in the same party, may be influencing each other. Thus, some of the influence attributed to senior senators in their junior partners' equations may result from the senior senators following their younger colleagues' positions. This is more likely to be true among the more senior pairs, such as Hill and Sparkman, Magnuson and Jackson, and Byrd (Va.) and Robertson, than for pairs where the junior member is a newcomer. In all cases where a simultaneous relationship was possible, the models were estimated with a procedure developed for simultaneous equations in addition to the ordinary regressions.[12] If a simultaneous relationship is present in any of these models it should be apparent in the co-efficients estimated by the simultaneous equation technique, in which case they are the appropriate estimates to use in evaluating the models of legislative voting behavior.

The final case in which simultaneous influences might be a problem is with the party leader variables in the individual equations. If the party leaders are influenced by sentiment within the Senate or within their own party, it means the individual senators exert an influence on the party leaders. Conceivably this makes ordinary regression estimates of the individual senators' models inappropriate. Of course, if the party leaders do not respond to these mean senator variables, there is no problem. Even if they do, the problem will not be very severe for individual senators. An individual senator is only one of at least thirty-six (the number of Republicans) and possibly of one hundred senators influencing the party leaders. Consequently the influence of any one senator over the party leader will be quite small and probably not systematic, and little or no harm is done using ordinary regression to estimate these models.[13]

There are many problems inherent in measuring senators' voting behavior and in estimating the influences on this behavior. Some of these problems are surmountable, as in the case of simultaneous influences. Other problems, such as the difficulties with the method used to construct the constituency variables and the use of Guttman scale variables in regression equations, can only be noted, with an attempt made to understand their effects. These effects are discussed briefly in this chapter and more fully in the appendixes. In spite of these difficulties, the results obtained from estimating these equations for individual senators should provide insights into the importance of different influences on legislative voting behavior and useful information about the different approaches to explaining it.

APPENDIX 3.1. LEGISLATIVE SCALES

	Bill number	Bill title	C.Q. roll calls[a]	C.R.[b]	M.M.R.[c]
1961					
1.	S 1	Area Redevelopment Act	5, 9, 10, 6, 7, 8	0.962	0.653
2.	HR 4806	Temporary Extended Unemployment Compensation	15, 16, 14, 17	0.978	0.673
3.	HR 4510	Emergency Feed Grains Act			
	HR 5188	Third Supplemental Appropriations			
	HR 7444	Appropriations for Department of Agriculture and Commodity Credit Corporation			
4.	S 1643	Agriculture Act of 1961 (amendment to eliminate extension of feed grains)	99, 4, 20, 78	0.928	0.665
	HR 3935	Fair Labor Standards Amendments of 1961 (dealing with extension of the minimum wage)	30, 29, 26, 31	0.987	0.593
5.	S 1021	School Assistance Act of 1961	54, 51, 53, 47	0.978	0.695
6.	S 1922	Housing Act of 1961			
	HR 7445	Appropriate Funds for Housing Research	68, 65, 62, 71, 74, 59, 58, 73, 75, 115	0.967	0.621
7.	S 1154	Educational and Cultural Exchange Act	93, 90, 91, 92, 89, 88, 96	0.977	0.680
8.	S 1643	Agriculture Act of 1961 (amendments to limit mergers of cooperatives and make them subject to antitrust laws)	101, 103, 102, 100, 98	0.963	0.590

APPENDIX 3.1. (continued)

	Bill number	Bill title	C.Q. roll calls[a]	C.R.[b]	M.M.R.[c]
9.	HR 7035	Appropriations for HEW (specifically NIH)	119, 121, 120, 118	0.982	0.649
10.		Amendments to various bills to extend aid to schools in areas "impacted" by federal installations	186, 185, 150, 123, 122	0.944	0.646
11.	S 1983	Foreign Assistance Act of 1961	148, 149, 137, 134, 146, 141, 130, 142, 139, 147, 151, 140	0.952	0.663
12.	S 1991	Manpower Development and Training Act	152, 153, 154, 155	0.985	0.598
13.	HR 7371	Amendments to State-Justice-Judiciary Appropriations Extending the Civil Rights Commission	161, 162, 160, 165	1.000	0.691
14.	S 174	Establish a National Wilderness Preservation	172, 173, 175	0.977	0.650
15.	S 2180	Establish a U.S. Arms Control and Disarmament Agency	177, 178, 179	0.990	0.657
16.	HR 2010	Amend and extend the Mexican Farm Labor Program	183, 201, 202, 181, 182, 184	0.971	0.626
17.	HR 8444	Establish voting machinery to permit D.C. residents to participate in presidential elections	195, 196, 197, 198	0.973	0.681

No.	Bill	Description	Roll calls		
18.		Various public works projects	56, 69, 97, 22, 169, 159, 12	0.967	0.801
1962					
1.	S 1241	College Facilities and Scholarship Aid	8, 7, 10, 9	0.951	0.687
2.	S J Res 29	Constitutional amendment to abolish poll taxes	21, 20, 22	0.993	0.667
3.	S 2768	Authorize the president to purchase U.N. bonds	25, 26, 28, 24, 23	0.976	0.770
4.	S 2750	Void literacy tests for people with greater than a sixth grade education	3, 37, 34, 35	0.965	0.665
5.	S 3225	Food and Agriculture Act of 1962	46, 47, 44, 45, 196, 43, 42, 144, 143, 146	0.972	0.671
6.	S 2965	Standby Public Works Act of 1962	52, 54, 60, 174, 59, 208	0.990	0.765
7.	S 2996	Foreign Assistance Act of 1962	94, 95, 65	0.983	0.640
8.	S 2996	Foreign Assistance Act of 1962	213, 61, 212, 64, 63	0.960	0.685
	HR 13175	Foreign Assistance Appropriation of 1962 (amendments relating specifically to Communist nations)			
9.	HR 10802	Interior Department Appropriations	66, 69, 68, 72	0.970	0.633
10.	HR 12154	Sugar Act Amendments of 1962	78, 86, 85, 79	0.952	0.785
11.	HR 10606	Public Welfare Amendments of 1962 (amendments trying to establish Medicare)	91, 92, 93	0.993	0.677
12.	HR 10904	Appropriations for HEW and Labor	99, 102, 97, 96	0.964	0.607

APPENDIX 3.1. (continued)

	Bill number	Bill title	C.Q. roll calls[a]	C.R.[b]	M.M.R.[c]
13.	HR 11040	Communications Satellite Act of 1962	142, 135, 116, 139	0.993	0.750
14.	HR 10650	Revenue Act of 1962 (revision amendments)	164, 161, 166, 151, 163 155	0.941	0.721
15.	HR 11970	Trade Expansion Act of 1962	178, 182, 181, 185, 180,188	0.985	0.713
16.	HR 7927	Amendments to a postal rate and federal pay raise bill to limit delivery of communist political propaganda through the mail	197, 198, 203	1.000	0.723
17.	HR 13175	Foreign Assistance Appropriations Act of 1962	213, 217, 211, 210 219	0.971	0.653
18.	S 2800	Extension of maritime ship construction subsidy, amendments to eliminate the west coast preferential rate of 6%			
	HR 12580	Appropriations for the west coast preferential subsidy	190, 221	0.954	0.682
1963					
1.	S Res. 9	Change cloture rule	4, 1, 3, 2	0.993	0.683
2.	S Res. 90	Increase committee sizes			
	S Res. 15	Authorization for Banking and Currency Committee			

52

No.	Bill	Description			
3.	S Res. 29	Authorizations for Commerce Committee	6, 5, 8, 7	0.988	0.758
	S 6	Mass Transportation Act of 1963	17, 18, 20, 11, 10, 13, 9, 19	0.965	0.652
4.	S 4	Establish a National Wilderness Preservation System	24, 22, 23, 25	0.983	0.703
5.	S 1	Youth Employment Act	27, 31, 32, 33, 26, 28	0.980	0.652
6.	Public Works				
	S 2	Water Resources Research Act			
	HR 6016	Authorization for river basin, flood control, and power projects	37, 36, 87, 88, 206	0.984	0.692
	HR 8667	Authorizations for river basin and reservoir projects	52, 51, 45, 54, 48, 56	0.982	0.617
7.	HR 4997	Establish a feed grain acreage control program	64, 63, 62	0.994	0.759
8.	HR 5389	Silver purchase repeal	91, 92, 90, 95	0.964	0.675
9.	HR 5888	Appropriations for Depts. of Labor and HEW	99, 104, 100	0.986	0.600
10.	S 1321	National Service Corps Act	109, 207, 93, 106	0.953	0.574
11.	S 1703	Extend Mexican farm labor program	115, 112, 113, 116	0.985	0.900
12.	S J Res. 102	Establish an arbitration board for railroad work rules dispute	118, 91, 120, 122, 117, 119, 121	0.982	0.687
13.	S 1716	Amend Manpower Development and Training Act			

APPENDIX 3.1. (continued)

	Bill number	Bill title	C.Q. roll calls[a]	C.R.[b]	M.M.R.[c]
14.	HR 12	Health Professions Education Assistance Act	124, 125, 126, 68		
	S 1576	Authorize grants for research, treatment, and construction program in mental health		0.985	0.792
15.	Exec. M.	Limited Nuclear Test Ban Treaty	132, 130, 133, 129, 128	0.990	0.808
16.	HR 7179	Appropriations for Dept. of Defense	134, 136, 135	0.993	0.787
17.	HR 6754	Appropriations for the Agriculture Dept.	141, 139, 142	0.983	0.803
18.	S 1066	Expand subsidy for fishing boat construction			
19.	S 927	Amend 1936 Merchant Marine Act	209, 145, 146	0.986	0.717
	HR 4955	Authorizations for vocational education	147, 149, 214	0.997	0.843
20.	S 1915	Authorize Sec. of Agriculture to set milk production allotments	150, 152, 151	0.986	0.658
21.	HR 6143	Authorize federal grants to colleges	155, 154, 211, 158	0.966	0.653
22.	HR 7885	Foreign Assistance Act of 1963 (funds for development and assistance)	183, 166, 164, 182, 190	0.968	0.576

54

23.	HR 7885	Foreign Assistance Act of 1963 (amendments to limit presidential discretion and extend requirements for assistance)	172, 171, 181, 185, 179, 184	0.970	0.707
24.	HR 8747	Independent Offices Appropriations (funds for NASA, the SST, and NSF)	196, 194, 193, 192, 198	0.980	0.735
25.	HR 8969	Extend temporary national debt limit of $309 billion, then raise it $315 billion			
	HR 6009	Increase temporary national debt limit to $307 billion, then $309 billion			
	HR 7824	Extend temporary national debt limit of $309 billion	199, 69, 200, 110, 70	0.980	0.624

[a]Order of roll calls indicates the order in the Guttman Scales.

[b]Coefficient of Reproducibility, the percentage of the total votes which fit the scale pattern.

[c]Coefficient of Marginal Reproducibility, the percentage of the total votes which should fit the scale based on the majority voting pattern on each vote.

APPENDIX 3.2. DISTRIBUTION OF SCALE SCORES FOR EACH BILL

Bill	Original													Rescaled				
	0	1	2	3	4	5	6	7	8	9	10	11	12	0	1	2	3	4
1961-1	18	7	8	4	8	5	50							18	7	12	13	50
1961-2	5	42	9	9	35									5	42	9	9	35
1961-3	19	9	13	5	54									19	9	13	5	54
1961-4	31	6	7	5	50									31	6	7	5	50
1961-5	11	17	10	7	55									11	17	10	7	55
1961-6	18	14	5	3	5	3	1	4	8	16	22			18	14	29	16	22
1961-7	5	15	10	8	9	4	14	34						5	15	31	14	34
1961-8	33	3	9	6	7	40								33	12	6	7	40
1961-9	22	8	11	5	53									22	8	11	5	53
1961-10	40	2	4	13	33	8								40	6	13	33	8
1961-11	11	11	6	3	6	5	5	3	4	3	14	19	12	11	20	38	19	12
1961-12	28	13	3	2	53									28	13	3	2	53
1961-13	19	2	33	7	37									19	2	33	7	37
1961-14	14	27	9	50										14	27		9	50*
1961-15	15	25	10	49										15	25		10	49*
1961-16	7	39	1	7	3	6	35							7	39	8	9	35
1961-17	7	29	15	9	34									7	29	15	9	34
1961-18	2	4	4	15	16	17	29	13						6	19	33	29	13
1962-1	12	8	25	2	52									12	8	25	2	52
1962-2	17	18	27	36										17	18	27		36*

Period					
1962-3	14	7	2	4	3
1962-4	31	23	15	5	26
1962-5	15	9	13	3	2
1962-6	5	6	18	16	8
1962-7	25	11	16	47	
1962-8	30	11	10	16	24
1962-9	30	14	9	21	26
1962-10	3	16	24	35	21
1962-11	6	38	9	47	45
1962-12	28	9	9	7	14
1962-13	62	10	8	6	9
1962-14	17	23	16	13	9
1962-15	13	3	7	7	
1962-16	20	41	9	25	
1962-17	29	5	14	25	22
1962-18	26	36	37		
1963-1	4	40	12	12	32
1963-2	21	5	54	5	15
1963-3	25	3	3	8	3
1963-4	12	17	6	9	56
1963-5	10	25	7	2	5
1963-6	21	4	3	5	4
1963-7	29	2	3	7	3
1963-8	66	8	10	15	
1963-9	12	8	18	24	35

Period					
1962-3	14	7	6	3	70
1962-4	31	23	15	5	26
1962-5	15	22	11	33	18
1962-6	5	24	24	43	4
1962-7	25	11	16	16	47*
1962-8	30	21	9	24	8
1962-9	30	14	24	21	26
1962-10	3	16		35	21
1962-11	6	38	9	9	47*
1962-12	28	9	8	7	45
1962-13	62	10	29	6	14
1962-14	17	23	16	15	14
1962-15	13	10		11	48
1962-16	20	41	14	9	25*
1962-17	29	5	36	25	22
1962-18	26				37
1963-1	4	40	12	12	32
1963-2	21	5	54	5	15
1963-3	25	14	13	42	5
1963-4	12	17	6	9	56
1963-5	10	25	14	29	21
1963-6	21	7	5	4	63
1963-7	29	5	10	8	48
1963-8	66	8		10	15*
1963-9	12	8	18	24	35

APPENDIX 3.2. (continued)

Bill	Original													Rescaled				
	0	1	2	3	4	5	6	7	8	9	10	11	12	0	1	2	3	4
1963-10	29	17	15	38										29	17		15	38*
1963-11	38	10	13	20	19									38	10	13	20	19
1963-12	2	12	71	13	2									2	12	71	13	2
1963-13	19	5	8	7	2	17	31	6						19	20	19	31	6
1963-14	3	8	12	30	45									3	8	12	30	45
1963-15	11	4	4	17	52	12								11	8	17	52	12
1963-16	6	5	37	52										6	5		37	52*
1963-17	4	18	12	66										4	18		12	66*
1963-18	19	2	22	57										19	2		22	57*
1963-19	6	4	19	71										6	4		19	71*
1963-20	18	27	21	29										18	27		21	29*
1963-21	25	5	10	19	38									25	5	10	19	38
1963-22	25	14	11	4	10	36								25	14	15	10	36
1963-23	6	16	12	14	19	16	17							6	28	33	16	17
1963-24	1	8	32	9	30	18								9	32	9	30	18
1963-25	26	5	4	13	1	51								26	5	4	14	51

*Actual values are 0, 1.33, 2.67, and 4.00.

[4] Voting Behavior of
Individual Senators

The results from estimating the individual senators' models are
presented in three parts. This chapter discusses the systematic
components of the voting equations—their fits for the 1961–62
data used to estimate the models and the relative importance of
the different variables in each senator's equation. The capacity of
these equations to explain the votes cast in 1963, which are not
used in estimating the models, is evaluated in the next chapter.
Finally, the deviations from the systematic models will be discussed for the individual pieces of legislation in Chapter 6.

THE INDIVIDUAL RESULTS

The procedure followed in estimating the individual models was
first to estimate an equation for each senator containing the
variables shown in Table 2.1. However, each senator's equation
will contain a number of unimportant variables which should be
statistically insignificant. This will be true even if the senator's
voting is best represented by a mixture of the explanations of
legislative behavior, and it certainly will be true if only one of the
explanations is appropriate. Consequently, after these initial
estimates were made, the equations were reestimated, deleting the

obviously insignificant variables.[1] The discussions in the remainder of the book refer to the coefficients obtained from the second set of estimated equations. This procedure, of course, runs the risk of excluding a variable which does, in fact, affect a senator's votes but which happened to have a low estimated coefficient in this data set. The distributions of the coefficients from the first equations with all the variables included are shown in an appendix to this chapter.

The Fits of the Individual Equations

The estimated equations for the individual senators were statistically significant and accounted for a high percentage of the variance in their 1961–62 voting scale scores, as measured by the R^2 from each equation. Table 4.1 shows the distribution of the R^2 values corrected for degrees of freedom for the five different groups of senators. These results can be interpreted to mean that the variables shown in Table 2.1 were explaining more than half of the observed variance in the voting behavior of 72 of the 101 senators and less than a third of the variance for only 7 of the senators. These distributions substantiate the statement that the postulated models accounted for a large proportion of most

TABLE 4.1. DISTRIBUTIONS OF THE R^2'S FOR EASTERN, SOUTHERN, AND WESTERN DEMOCRATS AND EASTERN AND WESTERN REPUBLICANS

Group	0.00–0.29	0.30–0.39	0.40–0.49	0.50–0.59	0.60–0.69	0.70–0.79	0.80–1.00	Number of senators
E. Dem.	2	2	1	9	8	–	1	23
S. Dem.	–	1	3	4	5	4	1	18
W. Dem.	4	3	7	2	4	3	–	23
E. Rep.	–	3	1	7	3	3	1	18
W. Rep.	1	–	1	6	7	–	4	19
Total	7	9	13	28	27	10	7	101

senators' voting behavior as measured by the Guttman scales. This is particularly notable when the range of legislation included in the data is considered. Only two models are not significant at the 0.05 level, as measured by the formal F-test. These are Senators Morse and Neuberger, both Democrats from Oregon.

It is interesting to note the generally poorer performance of the models for the western Democrats and better-than-average performance for the group of southern Democrats. Thirty-one percent of the western Democrats had R^2 values less than 0.40, compared to only 12 percent of the remaining senators. Twenty-eight percent of the southern Democrats had R^2 values greater than 0.70, while only 14 percent of the other senators had values that high. This may mean that influences excluded from the models are more prevalent among western Democrats and less so among southerners. Alternatively, the measurements of the western Democrats' positions may contain more errors or represent less systematic voting behavior than other senators' measures, while the measurements of southern senators' voting contains less of these disturbances.

Constituency Influence

The constituency variable is the most consistently significant influence. Table 4.2 presents the distributions of the constituency coefficients for the different groups of senators. These distributions indicate that the constituency variables had a large influence on senators' scale scores. This was particularly true for Republicans and southern Democrats, even though a large number of the western Republicans have statistically insignificant constituency coefficients. Over one half of the constituency coefficients for senators in these three groups exceed 0.80, and their mean coefficients are higher than those of the northern Democrats. Since the constituency variables are based on the Guttman scale scores and the dependent variables are the scale scores, these coefficients signify that a unit change in constituency position is associated with close to a unit change in the senator's voting behavior. This

TABLE 4.2. DISTRIBUTIONS OF CONSTITUENCY COEFFICIENTS

Group	Number insig.[a]	Number of senators with significant coefficients in each range					Mean values[b]	
		0.30– 0.49	0.50– 0.74	0.75– 0.99	1.00– 1.24	≥ 1.25	All coeff.	Signif. coeff.
E. Dem.	11(4)[c]	8	1	2	–	1	0.30	0.57
S. Dem.[d]	2(2)[c]	–	5	2	5	4	0.94	1.06
W. Dem.	8(2)[c]	4	5	4	2	–	0.47	0.70
E. Rep.	2(2)[c]	1	3	7	2	3	0.84	0.95
W. Rep.	7(3)[c]	–	–	8	1	3	0.66	1.04

[a]Insignificant at the 0.05 level for a two-tailed test.

[b]All coefficients refers to the mean computed over all senators. Significant coefficient refers to the mean computed with only the significant coefficients.

[c]The numbers in parentheses are the number of senators with insignificant constituency coefficients, but significant coefficients for the other senator from his state.

[d]The equations estimated for Sparkman and Hill contained only the exogenous variables shown in Table 2.1 (see subsequent discussion of senior senator variables).

suggests a very strong influence, and to the extent that the variable is accurately measuring constituency preferences, it indicates that constituencies were important influences on the voting behavior of Republicans and southern Democrats.

The distribution of constituency coefficients for the non-southern Democrats is markedly different from the distributions for the previous groups. Even excluding those senators with significant coefficients for the other senator from their state, over half of the nonsouthern Democrats have insignificant constituency coefficients or coefficients less than 0.50. This indicates that on a consistent basis constituencies were much less influential for senators in these two groups. These northern Democratic senators also gave more weight to the positions of the party leaders and committee members than did the southerners and Republicans. These northern Democrats were not following the strict constituency model as closely as Republicans and southern Democrats.

The Party Leaders

The most important organizational variables were the four variables measuring the formal party leaders—the majority and minority leaders and whips. Table 4.3 presents the distributions of the coefficients on these variables.[2] The varying amounts of the party floor leaders' influence is very apparent in these results. Forty percent of the nonsouthern Democrats have significant coefficients for either Senator Mansfield, the majority leader, or Senator Humphrey, the majority whip. (Randolph was the only senator with significant coefficients for both leaders). A majority of the significant coefficients are larger than 0.50, and one is as high as 1.10, which further reveals the effectiveness of the Democratic leadership among the nonsoutherners during this session.

Mansfield's influence was actually more extensive than indicated by these coefficients. This can be seen by considering the set of senators not affected by Mansfield directly but who were influenced by Humphrey, who in turn was influenced by Mansfield. (Mansfield's coefficient in Humphrey's model is 0.33.) Thus,

TABLE 4.3. DISTRIBUTION OF COEFFICIENTS FOR PARTY LEADERS AND WHIPS

Group	Number insig.[a]	Number of senators with significant coefficients in each range								Mean values[b]	
		≤ -0.50	-0.25 -0.49	0.00 -0.24	0.25- 0.49	0.50- 0.74	0.75- 0.99	≥ 1.00	Tot. > 0	All coeff.	Signif. coeff.
E. Dem. (23)											
Leader	18	—	1	1[c]	2	1	—	—	4	0.06	0.37
Whip	14[d]	—	—	—	4[c]	1	2	1	8	0.23	0.65
S. Dem. (18)											
Leader	17	1	—	—	—	—	—	—	0	0.00	0.00
Whip	18	—	—	—	—	—	—	—	0	0.00	0.00
W. Dem. (23)											
Leader	16[e]	—	—	1	2	3	—	—	6	0.13	0.48
Whip	20[e]	—	—	—	—	2	—	—	2	0.06	0.64
E. Rep. (18)											
Leader	14	—	—	—	3	1	—	—	4	0.10	0.44
Whip	17	—	—	1	—	—	—	—	1	0.01	0.22
W. Rep. (19)											
Leader	12[f]	—	2	1	3	—	—	—	4	0.08	0.35
Whip	17[f,g]	—	—	—	—	—	—	—	0	0.00	0.00

[a]Coefficient not significant at the 0.05 level for a two-tailed test.
[b]The mean values only include the positive coefficients.
[c]Senator Randolph (D., W.Va.) had significant coefficients for both Mansfield and Humphrey.
[d]Senator Humphrey excluded from total.
[e]Senator Mansfield excluded from total.
[f]Senator Dirksen excluded from total.
[g]Senator Kuchel excluded from total.

18 of the 44 nonsouthern Democrats, excluding Mansfield and Humphrey, were directly responsive to the positions of these two leaders. For those nonsouthern Democrats with significant coefficients for the party leadership, Humphrey seems to be more influential among senators from eastern states and Mansfield more so among western senators, influence being assessed by the number of senators with significant coefficients.

In direct contrast to Mansfield and Humphrey is the influence of Dirksen and Kuchel, their Republican counterparts. The Republican party leaders have significant positive coefficients in the models of only a fourth of the Republicans. This is still below the Democratic leaders' percentage if the comparison is made for all Democrats, not just the nonsouthern Democratic ones. Including all Democrats means that 19 of 62 Democrats (31 percent) and 9 of 35 Republicans (26 percent) had significant coefficients for one or both party leaders. Only one of the nine Republican coefficients exceeds 0.50, compared to half of the significant coefficients for the nonsouthern Democrats. More importantly, the coefficient on Dirksen's vote in Kuchel's model is only 0.22 with a standard error of 0.17. Thus, at most confidence levels, the hypothesis that Dirksen exerted no influence on Kuchel cannot be rejected. In turn, Kuchel had virtually no apparent consistent influence among other members of his party. These two circumstances constitute a weakness in the Republican party senatorial organization. Compare these estimates with the Democrats, where Mansfield's coefficient in Humphrey's model was 0.33 with a standard error of 0.09, and Humphrey himself has significant coefficients in as many other models as Mansfield does.[3]

The antipathy of southern Democrats towards the Senate leadership of their national party is apparent. Neither Mansfield nor Humphrey enters any of their equations with a statistically significant positive coefficient (the negative leader coefficient is on Mansfield in Russell's equation). Coincident with this lack of influence by the party leaders, the southern Democrats exhibit

very strong constituency coefficients, both in statistical significance and in magnitude. In an interview early in the study, a
former aide to Senators Randolph and Morse and legislative
specialist for the Labor Department cited the eastern Republicans
and southern Democrats as the groups most responsive to their
constituencies.[4] This seems to be born out both by the relative
size of the constituency coefficients for these senators and by the
lack of statistical significance for most of the leadership variables
included in their voting models.

The models proposed for the two party floor leaders, Mansfield
and Dirksen, contain the positions of the average senator and the
average member of each party as explanatory variables. This
follows the arguments of Truman that the party leaders take
positions which accommodate the distributions of interests within
the Senate or within their parties.[5] These pressures are represented
by the mean scale score on each bill of all senators, and of the
Republican and the Democratic senators. The mean senator and
mean Democrat variables are included in alternative versions of
Mansfield's equation, and the mean Republican variable in
Dirksen's equation. The equations containing these variables are
estimated by the simultaneous equation procedure discussed in
Chapter 3. The results, although not statistically significant, are
consistent with Truman's hypotheses. All three variables have
positive coefficients in these equations. The magnitudes of these
coefficients range from 0.40 for the mean senator variable to
0.50 for the mean Democrat and mean Republican variables. In
each case, however, the standard errors of these coefficients are as
large or larger than the coefficients. When the other statistically
insignificant variables are deleted from Mansfield's and Dirksen's
equations, the coefficients on the mean seantor and mean party
variables increase by 0.10. However only the statistical significance
of the mean Democratic variable changes appreciably. The coefficient is still not significant at the 5 percent level, but it is
significant at the 10 percent level (the t-statistic is 1.80 in this

case). Thus, there is only minor statistical support for Truman's hypotheses that the party leaders are influenced by the distribution of opinion within their parties.[6]

The positions of the committee chairman and ranking minority committee member are also included in Mansfield's and Dirksen's equations, respectively. This should test another of Truman's hypotheses which is that the party leaders are influenced by the party's seniority leaders.[7] The committee chairman's coefficient in Mansfield's equation is quite small, never greater than 0.10, and has a very large standard error, never less than 0.11. The coefficient on the ranking minority committee member in Dirksen's equation is on the order of 0.40 and statistically significant at the 5 percent level. These results support Truman's notions for Dirksen, but not for Mansfield. However this result runs counter to Truman's statement that the seniority leaders will be more influential in the majority party.[8]

The Committee Leaders

There is support for the argument that senators are influenced by positions taken by leading members of the reporting committee. One-third of all senators have significant positive coefficients for either the committee chairman, ranking minority member, committee liberal, or committee conservative variables. These coefficients are shown in Table 4.4. Half of these coefficients are for a member of the committee other than the chairman or ranking minority member. These senators are chosen for their ideological identifications and presumably have less political leverage, in the traditional sense, than the seniority leaders. Their influence is based largely on their positions as experts, or as representatives of coalitions within each party. It should also be pointed out that the committee liberal and committee conservative variables are more important than the committee chairman and ranking minority member variables as measured by the size of the coefficients. Neither of these committee member variables have much influence

TABLE 4.4. COEFFICIENTS FOR THE COMMITTEE VARIABLES

Group	Number insig.[a]	Number of senators with significant coefficients in each range								Mean values[b]	
		-0.25- -0.49	0.00- -0.24	0.00- 0.24	0.25- 0.49	0.50- 0.74	0.75- 1.00	≥ 1.00	Tot. > 0	All coeff.	Signif. coeff.
E. Dem.											
Chairman	20	1	1[c]	1	–	–	–	–	1	0.01	0.22
Liberal	15	–	–	–	3	2	2	1[c]	8	0.25	0.64
S. Dem.											
Chairman	13	–	1	1	3	–	–	–	4	0.06	0.28
W. Dem.											
Chairman	15	–	1	4	2	1	–	–	7	0.08	0.27
Liberal	22	–	–	–	–	1	–	–	1	0.03	0.60
E. Rep. Ranking											
Rep.	16	–	–	2	–	–	–	–	2	0.01	0.09
Cons.	17	–	–	–	1	–	–	–	1	0.02	0.44
W. Rep. Ranking											
Rep.	14	–	–	2	3[d]	–	–	–	5	0.07	0.26
Cons.	13	–	–	–	2	1	1[d]	2	6	0.23	0.73

[a]Coefficients insignificant at the 0.05 level for a two-tailed test.
[b]Only includes significant positive coefficients.
[c]Senator Douglas had significant coefficients for both the Committee Chairman and Committee Liberal.
[d]Senator Bennett had significant coefficients for both the Ranking Committee Republican and Committee.

among eastern Republicans. (The two coefficients shown for eastern Republicans for the ranking minority member are barely significant at the 0.05 level.)

There is a noticeable difference in the geographic distribution of the committee chairman's and committee liberal's influences. The number of significant positive coefficients for the committee chairman variable is virtually confined to Democrats from the Rocky Mountain and southwestern states, while only one senator from these states (Church) has a statistically significant coefficient for the committee liberal variable. Conversely, the committee chairman variable has two significant negative coefficients and only one small positive coefficient in the eastern Democrats' models, while the committee liberal variable is statistically significant in eight of their models. This is hardly surprising considering that all but one of the committee chairmen were southerners or southwesterners during these two years.

It is surprising, though, that the committee chairman variable is not statistically significant in more southern Democrats' equations. One possible explanation for this unexpected result is that the southern committee chairmen were either quite liberal southerners, such as Hill and Sparkman, or quite conservative like Byrd (Va.) and Eastland, as measured by their mean scale scores for the thirty-six scales. Most committee chairmen may have been voting certain ideological or constituency positions which were not followed by the other southerners. Other explanations for the overall results for the southern Democrats are offered later.

The least significant influence included in the basic equations is that of the chairman of the Republican Policy Committee, which is included in the Republican's equations. This variable is not significantly positive in any Republican senator's equation. In all the equations, the coefficient on the Policy Committee variable is quite small and insignificant. In part this could be due to the change in the chairmanship of this committee when Senator Styles Bridges died between sessions and was replaced by Senator Hickenlooper. If some senators were influenced by Bridges but

not Hickenlooper, or vice versa, it could lead to small coefficients
for the Policy Committee Chairman variable. It also indicates,
however, that it was not the formal position of the chairman
among the party leadership which is important if this influence
is not transferred when the chairmanship changes. It seems that the
Policy Committee chairman's position is not an influential one
on a consistent basis.

The President

The final influence expected to be consistently important in
senators' voting behavior is the position of the president. The
two variables measuring the president's positions do not appear to
be very important. Table 4.5 shows the distributions of the
presidential position variable coefficients. The presidential position
variable is significant in eight nonsouthern Democrats' and three
Republicans' models. It has a positive coefficient in two of the
Republican models, Prouty and Case (New Jersey), and in seven of
the eight Democratic ones. The northern Democrat with a negative
coefficient is Gruening. However, only the presidential dummy

TABLE 4.5. DISTRIBUTION OF COEFFICIENTS FOR PRESIDENTIAL
POSITION VARIABLE

Group	Number insig.[a]	Number of senators with significant coefficients in each range				Mean values[b]	
		−0.25−−0.49	0.00−−0.24	0.00−0.24	0.25−0.49	All coeff.	Signif. coeff.
E. Dem. (23)	19	—	—	1	3	0.06	0.36
S. Dem. (18)	14	2	1	—	1	0.02	0.47
W. Dem. (23)	19	—	1	1	2	0.03	0.25
E. Rep. (18)	16	—	—	1	1	0.03	0.26
W. Rep. (19)	18	1	—	—	—	0.00	0.00

[a]Coefficient not significant at the 0.05 level for a two-tailed test.
[b]Only includes significant positive coefficients.

variable enters either of the Democratic floor leaders' models with even marginal statistical significance. It is significant in Mansfield's model and indicates that Mansfield took a more liberal position if the president had not taken a position. Mr. Sundquist had argued that the positions taken by Mansfield and Humphrey were essentially the administration's positions.[9] Although this is an oversimplification, it does suggest that the presidential variable should be statistically significant in their models. These coefficients' lack of significance casts more doubt on the construction of the variables than on the hypotheses themselves. The *Congressional Quarterly's* assessment of the president's public statements to determine his being for, against, or neutral on each vote undoubtedly did not adequately measure the information Mansfield or Humphrey received about the president's feelings towards each amendment and bill. Mansfield and Humphrey were probably responding to more subtle information on the president's position which is not measured by the variables used here. These erroneous measures would lead to an underestimate of presidential influence. The only solution is to try to find additional information which will permit the inclusion of these subtleties.

The results for other senators suggest a small amount of presidential influence exerted directly on individual senators. These results could also be effected by poor measures of President Kennedy's positions, though. However, the results for the party leaders, along with Mr. Sundquist's hypothesis, strongly suggest that there is a considerable amount of presidential influence but that it is exerted through the formal party structure.

Informal Leaders: The Senior Colleagues

One of the best confirmed informal leaders hypotheses was that of the influence of a senior senator on his junior partner if both are in the same party. In seventeen cases the senior senator has a significant positive coefficient in the junior's model and in two others has a significant negative coefficient. These coefficients are shown in Table 4.6.

TABLE 4.6. DISTRIBUTION OF COEFFICIENTS FOR SENIOR SENATOR HYPOTHESIS[a]

Group	Number insig.[b]	≤ -0.50	-0.25 / -0.49	0.00- 0.24	0.25- 0.49	0.50- 0.74	0.75- 0.99	≥ 1.00	All pairs	Signif. pairs
		Number of senators with significant coefficients in each range							Mean values	
E. Dem. (6)[c]	2	—	—	—	1	3	—	—	0.42	0.63
S. Dem. (9)[d]	6	—	—	—	1	1	1	—	0.23	0.71
W. Dem. (6)[e]	5	—	—	—	1	1	—	—	0.07	0.42
E. Rep. (7)	2	1	1	—	1	—	—	1	0.29	0.69
W. Rep. (5)	1[f]	—	—	—	1	—	3	—	0.62	0.79

[a]Entries are the coefficient of the senior senator in the junior's model. Totals refer only to possible senior-junior pairs in the same party, not all senators.
[b]Coefficient not significantly different from zero at the 0.05 level for a two-tailed test.
[c]The effect of Humphrey on McCarthy is excluded.
[d]The effect of Hill on Sparkman is included.
[e]The effect of Mansfield on Metcalf is excluded.
[f]Insignificant pair is Curtis-Hruska. See Discussion in text.

The only consistent exceptions to this hypothesis are among the southern and western Democrats. The other exceptions are Lausche-Young (Ohio) and Byrd-Randolph (W.Va.) among the eastern Democrats, and Morton-Cooper (Ky.) and Beall-Butler (Md.) among the Republicans. The only ones with negative coefficients are Bridges-Cotton (N.H.), for 1961 while Bridges was alive, and Williams-Boggs (Del.). In addition to the feelings of personal loyalty or the need for guidance by newer members mentioned by Matthews,[10] the existence or absence of a strong state party and each senator's role in that party may explain some of the results. The absence of cohesive state parties in the south and to some extent in the west, as compared to the east and midwest, may explain the failure of this hypothesis in these areas. One southern pair where the hypothesis is confirmed, that of Byrd and Robertson (Va.), certainly is consistent with this explanation considering the existence of the so-called Byrd machine.

These senior-junior influences are examples of relationships where simultaneity is suspected. This possibility is tested in five different cases using the procedure developed for reciprocal influences. The five cases were Magnuson and Jackson (D., Wash.), McNamara and Hart (D., Mich.), Hill and Sparkman (D., Ala.), Schoeppel and Carlson (R., Kans.), and Hruska and Curtis (R., Nebr.). In three cases, the coefficient for the effect of the junior senator on the senior senator is zero, or very close to it, and is not statistically significant, while the effect of the senior on the junior senator is large and statistically significant. Senators Magnuson and Jackson (D., Wash.) provide an excellent example of this result. Equations 4.1 and 4.2 are the appropriate simultaneous equation estimates of their models.

$$(4.1) \quad \text{Magnuson} = \quad -0.89 \; + \; 0.42 \, \text{Washington} + \; 0.67 \, \text{Humphrey}$$
$$\phantom{(4.1) \quad \text{Magnuson} = } (0.96) \quad (0.26) \phantom{\text{Washington} +} (0.27)$$
$$\phantom{(4.1) \quad \text{Magnuson} = } + \; 0.08 \, \text{Jackson} R^2 = 0.54$$
$$\phantom{(4.1) \quad \text{Magnuson} = } (0.96)$$

(4.2)   Jackson = 1.33 + 0.26 Mansfield + 0.37 Magnuson $R^2 = 0.47$
                (0.51)   (0.13)   (0.17)

(standard errors in parentheses)

The significant point is that when the appropriate procedure is used, the hypothesized influence of Jackson, the junior senator, on Magnuson is both small and statistically insignificant. The reverse relationship, that of Magnuson on Jackson, is large and statistically significant. The conclusion is that this is not a simultaneous relationship and that both senators' models can be estimated using the ordinary regression technique with Jackson omitted from Magnuson's equation.

One interesting aberration is Curtis and Hruska (R., Nebr.). In the appropriate estimations only the influence of Curtis on Hruska was significant. Technically Hruska is the senior senator, although these two men came into the Senate less than two months apart, Hruska on November 8, 1954 and Curtis on January 1, 1955. However, both are former members of the House, Curtis for sixteen years and Hruska for only two. Thus, prior to coming to the Senate, Curtis was clearly the senior person. Consequently, the formal definitions of senior and junior senator are concluded to have broken down in this case.

The only exception to this pattern among the five pairs is Senators Hill and Sparkman of Alabama. In this case both senators appear to influence each other. Each of these two had been in the Senate a long time and was an anomaly among the other southern senators as far as the liberalness of their voting records is concerned. For these reasons, it is anticipated that there would be a considerable amount of discussion and interaction between these two and a breakdown of the formal senior-junior role. In spite of this breakdown, Hill, the senior, seemed to have had a larger effect on Sparkman, the junior, than vice versa when both were estimated by the simultaneous equation method. These estimations are quite uncertain, however. Meaningful simultaneous equation estimates of each senator's structural equation showing the direct effects of each variable, such as constituency and the state partner, are difficult to obtain due to the tremendous similarity in their voting records. Consequently all the results reported hereafter refer to the equations estimating the total effect of each variable, called the reduced form.[11] These reduced form equations contain the standard variables for southern Democrats.

The senior senator influences substantially increase the amount of constituency influence over that shown in Table 4.2. In only one of the cases where a senator was influenced by his partner was this partner not substantially influenced by their constituency. This was McNamara (Mich.). In the other eighteen cases, the constituency coefficients are quite large. Thus, even though many of the junior senators have small and insignificant constituency coefficients, the total constituency effect is important when measured by the effect constituency has on the senior senator and the senior's influence on the junior partner. Table 4.7 shows the distribution of the direct constituency influences among those senators with significant senior senator coefficients and the estimated total effect which constituency had on their votes. This latter estimate is computed as the direct constituency coefficient *plus* the senior senator's coefficient times the constituency co-efficient in the senior's equation. The mean constituency effects for each group of senators are also shown. These distributions and means indicate that even though the junior senators' constituency coefficients imply that constituency has only a small direct effect on their voting behavior, it has a substantial total effect when the effect of the senior senator variable is considered.

Informal Leaders: Regional and Ideological

The influence of the regional and informal leaders was the hardest to include in the models because of the difficulty in obtaining information about which informal leaders belong in each equation. Several possibilities were mentioned and tested and can be evaluated. The most notable unsupported hypothesis is

TABLE 4.7. DIRECT AND TOTAL CONSTITUENCY INFLUENCE ON SENATORS WITH SIGNIFICANT STATE COLLEAGUE COEFFICIENTS

Group	Direct effect						Total effect					
	Insig.	0.25 0.49	0.50 0.74	0.75 0.99	≥1.00	Mean	0.00 0.24	0.25 0.49	0.50 0.74	0.75 0.99	≥1.00	Mean
E. Dem.	4	1	—	—	—	0.08	2	1	1	1	—	0.41
S. Dem.	2[a]	—	—	—	—	0.00	—	—	1	1	—	0.76
W. Dem.	2	—	—	—	—	0.00	1	1	—	—	—	0.33
E. Rep.	2	—	1	1	1	0.63	—	1	—	2	2	0.83
W. Rep.	3[b]	1	—	—	1	0.32	—	1	1	—	3	1.08

[a]Excludes Hill and Sparkman.
[b]Includes the effects of Curtis on Hruska.

the expected influence of a senior southern senator, notably
Senator Russell, among his southern colleagues. Russell does not
have a significant, positive coefficient in any of the southern
Democratic senators' equations. There are several conceivable
explanations for these results. If all the southerners voted as a very
cohesive group on all or most bills, down to the last amendment,
then these effects would be included in the constituency variable.
If all eighteen senators voted the same way, the effect of a Russell
would be contained in the coefficient of any variable in the constituency model that was highly correlated with "southness,"
such as the regional dummy. This would overstate the importance
of constituency and understate the role of personal leaders within
the Senate. This explanation is supported by the arguments in
Appendix A that the procedures used to estimate the constituency
variables could lead to an overstatement of constituency influence
and an understatement of leaders' influences. These biases are more
severe in cases where there was a strong correlation between a
leader's effects and the variables used to construct the constituency
variables. If Russell had an important effect on southern senators'
voting behavior, these effects would be correlated with the southern variables in the constituency equations, thus leading to an
understatement of Russell's influence.

An alternative explanation is that the observed bloc voting is
the effect of similar constituencies, not adroit political leadership.
In this case, the senators who are popularly mentioned as the
leaders of the southern group were spokesmen rather than cue-
givers or extremely powerful solons, as they have been characterized. Thus, Russell was a spokesman for the southern senators,
who arrived at the same positions because they were the products
of and represented similar social environments. In this model, the
publicized leaders are actually acting as the strategists or spokesmen for a group that already exists rather than the force which
creates the group.

Finally, the concept of a monolithic southern bloc on all bills
could be a myth. This stereotype could have been generated if

one or two types of legislation on which the eighteen senators were in general agreement received a disproportionate amount of national attention, even though they significantly diverged on other issues. This could create the popular impression of a solid bloc, with the spokesmen on the few convergent issues appearing to exert significant influence among this group of senators.

Reality may consist largely of the latter two explanations, although the possibility of the first is not excluded given the discussion in Appendix A. There is considerable evidence in the overall voting patterns of southern senators to indicate that they were not a monolithic bloc. The individual mean-scale scores for all bills range from 0.40 for Strom Thurmond (D., S.C.) to 2.88 for John Sparkman (D., Ala.). In fact, if civil rights bills are excluded, Hill and Sparkman had voting records as liberal as many nonsouthern Democrats, which was not true for Thurmond or Byrd (Va.). There is a fairly even distribution of scale scores between Thurmond's and Sparkman's positions, with only a slight concentration between 1.0 and 1.3. This analysis is consistent with V. O. Key's conclusion that, "on the race question, and on that question alone, does a genuine southern solidarity exist. On other questions southern Democrats split and southern solidarity becomes a matter of degree."[12]

This description supports the third explanation that "the bloc" was cohesive on a few bills which may have received a disproportionate amount of publicity. In such cases, the supposed leader is functioning as a tactician rather than an influential leader. Southern senators probably had very little trouble deciding how their constituencies felt about the Civil Rights Commission, and they needed little pressure from a Russell or an Eastland to vote against its extension.

There were several other informal leader hypotheses which are supported, however. A hypothesis suggested by Huitt's description of Senator Proxmire's decision to be an "outsider" in the Senate —"he would be a senator like Wayne (Morse) and Paul (Douglas)"[13] —is that Douglas might be an important explanatory variable in Proxmire's model. This was substantiated. The Douglas variable is quite statistically significant in Proxmire's equation, with a coefficient of 0.54. The hypothesis suggested by Mr. Sundquist, shown in Table 2.1, that Senator Kerr (D., Okla.) was influential in how Senator McCarthy (D., Minn.) voted is tested and found to be statistically significant, although the coefficient, which equalled 0.15, is not very large.

There are several ways to summarize the information about the voting behavior of individual senators. The right hand column in each table of coefficients shows the mean coefficient value for each group of senators. These mean values can be interpreted as a composite model for senators in each group. These composite models permit a comparison of the influence of constituencies and of the different leaders on these average senators. For example, the constituency influence on an eastern Democrat (0.30) is much less than that for a Republican (0.84 or 0.66) or a southern Democrat (0.94). Similarly, the Democratic party whip has almost as much influence among eastern Democrats as does their constituencies, 0.23 compared to 0.30. However these comparisons do not give an indication of the structure of the model followed by different senators.

It is the number of senators best represented by a constituency only model or a party leader only model that is important in evaluating the various approaches to studying legislative behavior. This information on the structure of the different models is summarized in Table 4.8. Table 4.8 shows the number of senators best described by the different models. In constructing this table, the floor leaders' and whips' effects and the influences of the two committee variables in each party are grouped together into single leadership and committee influences. In most cases comparison with earlier tables will make apparent which particular variable dominates the summary variable. Where a senator has significant coefficients for a different set of variables than those shown in Table 4.8, the pattern of the most important variables, as measured by the size of the coefficients, is used to characterize the

TABLE 4.8. MODEL SPECIFICATIONS

Group	Constit. only	Leader only	Committ. only	Constit./ leader	Constit./ committ.	Constit./ pres.	Constit./ leader/ committ.	Constit./ committ./ pres.
E. Dem.[a]	2	5[b]	3[c]	3	2	–	4	3[c]
S. Dem.	10	–	–	1	2	2[d]	–	3[d]
W. Dem.[a]	5	3[b]	–	4	4	3	1	–
E. Rep.	8	–	–	4	3	2	1	–
W. Rep.	5	–	4[c]	4	5	–	1	–

[a]Senators Smith (Mass.) and Moss (Utah) excluded because none of their significant coefficients fit the patterns and Morse and Neuberger are excluded because none of their coefficients were significant.

[b]McCarthy (Minn.) and Metcalf (Mont.) are included in the leadership category, although one of the party leaders is each senator's senior partner.

[c]The committee liberal or committee conservative variables were the important ones for all senators in these categories.

[d]Only one of these five presidential influences was positive. That was for Olin Johnston (S.C.).

senator. Except for the influence of senior senators, which is used to estimate the total constituency influence on each junior partner, the effects of regional and ideological leaders are excluded.

The dominance of constituency only models among only eastern Republicans and southern Democrats is apparent here. Leader only models are observed only for the nonsouthern Democrats. Committee chairman/ranking minority leader and committee liberal/conservative only models are observed among the eastern Democrats and western Republicans. The nonconstituency influences among the northern Democrats are quite evenly spread among the leadership and the committee members, while the committee variables are the most important nonconstituency influences among southern Democrats and western Republicans.

INDIVIDUAL MODELS AND EXPLANATIONS OF LEGISLATIVE BEHAVIOR

The remainder of this chapter will evaluate these results in terms of the support given to each of the different legislative voting models. In general, there was some evidence consistent with all the approaches except an individualistic or trusteeship one, while no one approach was confirmed completely. The fact that the statistical models explained a high proportion of most senators' voting behavior is inconsistent with an explanation based on the notion that senators' votes are the product of individual experiences and philosophies and cannot be related to a set of systematic influences.

The Formal-Leader Organizational Explanation

There is little evidence to support the strongest versions of the formal leader explanations of legislative behavior. Only eight senators, all northern Democrats, were best represented by a leader only equation. However there is strong support for the assertion that leaders are important. The floor leaders' and whips' variables are important in a quarter of the Republicans' and two-fifths of the northern Democrats' models. For eastern Democrats, these formal leaders were as influential as the senators' constituencies in terms of the number of significant coefficients and their magnitudes. If the southern senators are excluded, the Democratic leaders were more influential than their Republican counterparts, as measured both by the number of significant coefficients among the nonsoutherners and by the size of the significant coefficients. This is expected, both because the Democrats were the majority party in Congress and controlled the White House and because they had the more centralized leadership.

The real significant leadership difference, however, is between the influence of Humphrey and Kuchel rather than between Mansfield and Dirksen. Both Mansfield and Dirksen have significant coefficients in 20 to 25 percent of the equations for the other senators in their respective parties, exclusive of southern Democrats. Humphrey, however, has a significant coefficient in as many models as Mansfield, while Kuchel only has a significant coefficient in one other senator's model, and this coefficient was small and barely significant at the 5 percent level.

The difference in the number of senators influenced by the party whips and the fact that Mansfield had a significant coefficient in Humphrey's model while Dirksen did not in Kuchel's reflects the difference in party organizations and personalities. The differences in the leadership structure of each party and the difficulties created by the competition among Republicans for these posts has been discussed by Truman.[14] In addition, there were several suggestions that Mansfield and Humphrey worked together much better than Dirksen and Kuchel did. One former aide to Senator Kuchel said "That Dirksen would get up and 'Take him (Kuchel) to the woodshed' right on the senate floor for some of his positions."[15] Not only is this statement indicative of a distant relationship between leader and whip, but it does not seem designed to promote effective leadership through the whip's office, and it is hard to imagine Mansfield doing this to Humphrey.

The large number of significant constituency coefficients and the significant committee liberal and committee conservative co-

efficients are inconsistent with an approach completely emphasizing the formal leaders. If Senate voting were all a function
of internal influences dominated by the formal leaders, as the
organizational explanations emphasize and as the responsible
parties advocates say it should be, then the constituency and the
nonseniority committee member variables should not be statistically significant. The fact that they were indicates that models
relying solely on the behavior of the formal party leaders is an
inadequate and a misspecified model of Senate voting behavior.

The Cue-Source Organizational Model

These results, except for the constituency coefficients, actually
provide more support for the limited information version of the
internal view of the Senate. Proponents of this view of the voting
process, which is most associated with Matthews and Stimpson,
argue that the only way senators can obtain enough information
to cast rational votes is to see how other members, who are more
informed about each bill, are going to vote. The other, more
informed legislators are the formal, informal, and ideological
leaders, the senior members of the state or regional delegations,
and the recognized experts in the substantive field to which the
bill relates. The results, with significant coefficients for the committee liberal and conservative variables, the senior senator and
several of the informal leader variables, such as Douglas and Kerr,
as well as the formal leader variables, supports this view of legislative voting. The relative lack of significant coefficients for the
presidential variable is consistent with this model, since it is
difficult for undecided senators to consult the president on his
various public statements on their way to the floor to vote.
However, the overwhelming significance of the constituency
variables, and the fact that constituencies are about the only
significant variables for most southerners and eastern Republicans
casts doubt on this as an adequate model of Senate voting. It is
impossible for senators to ascertain how their constituencies, or
even individual constituents, feel about a bill in the simple deci-

sion process argued for by Matthews and Stimpson. Senators must have a conception of their constituents' positions and of how legislation will affect them by the time floor votes are taken. Otherwise there would not be as many significant constituency coefficients as there are.[16] This discussion does not mean that senators do not consult their colleagues for information about the content and potential consequences of a bill, or about how a bill may affect different constituencies. Once this information has been obtained, however, individual senators are capable of translating it into a constituency-oriented position and then deciding whether or not to support that position. The results indicate that many senators do not rely on their expert colleagues for directions on how to vote.

The Establishment Explanation

There is little support in these results for White's inner club view of the Senate. The important variables in this description are the more senior Senate establishment figures. These are generally argued to be the southern committee chairmen, ranking eastern Republican minority members, several informal leaders in these groups, such as Russell, and to some extent the formal party leaders. The fact that the committee chairman, ranking minority member, and Senator Russell variables are significant in only a few senators' models, while the constituency variables are more often significant with larger coefficients, creates serious doubts about the viability of this explanation for roll call voting on a consistent basis. This doubt is made even stronger by the absence of these hypothesized influences among southern Democrats and eastern Republicans who are supposed to be charter members of the "club."

The Representational Explanation

The pure representational explanations, such as the majoritarian explanation examined by Miller and Stokes and the intensity model of MacRae (who did include a party variable), appear to be inadequate for describing Senate roll call voting. Even though the constituency variable is the single most important one and has many more statistically significant coefficients than the other variables, it is not the only important influence. A more serious problem for the previous constituency only studies than just the fact that the organizational variables are statistically significant is that the coefficients on the leader variables exhibit a pattern which is correlated with most constituency measures. For example, the coefficients on the Humphrey and committee liberal variables are larger among eastern Democrats, while the Mansfield and committee chairman variables have their larger coefficients among the western Democrats, and all of these coefficients are small for southerners. Similarly, the variables representing Republican committee members generally have higher coefficients for the midwestern and western members than they do for the eastern members. The mere fact that the party leaders were influential, when combined with the simple observation that congressmen's party affiliations are quite likely correlated with the characteristics of their constituencies, means that any model with only constituency variables has a serious omitted variable problem. The impact of these omitted variables will be to bias the estimated effects of constituency positions, just as models which omit the constituency variable overestimate the influence of the organizational variables that are highly correlated with congressmen's constituencies' positions. The inclusion of a party dummy variable will improve this situation somewhat, but not completely, because there are regional and other variations in the leaders' and committees' influences within each party. These leadership effects and their association with regional and other constituency characteristics will also lead to some bias in the coefficients presented here. This problem is pointed out in Chapter 3 and is discussed in Appendix A. However the simple simulation presented in Appendix A implies that the correlation between the actual and the expected estimated coefficients is quite high, indicating that comparisons among legislators will still be valid if the simulation is representative. If the leadership variables are omitted altogether, the biases will be more serious.

The Behavioral Coalition Model

The results here are most consistent with the behavioral version of the coalition representational model, which formally includes both the constituency and leadership variables. The essence of this view of legislative voting is that most representatives know what issues are important to their constituents, and they try to obtain passage of the desired policies on these important issues. Legislators also understand that the best way to obtain these policies is to use their votes on less important issues to obtain other representatives' support on the more important issues. At the same time, most legislators realize that it is a more efficient use of their time and resources to join some organized coalition with a few leaders who arrange these trades and even represent the group in making arrangements with other such coalitions. Each of the parties, then, is just an organized coalition, and the formal leaders' responsibilities are to know what issues are important to each member and to deliver most of the party's votes on each bill. In addition, because these parties are so large, subcoalitions are likely to form within each one. These may form around one of the formal party leaders, such as the party whip, or simply around a group of legislators who form their own group and develop their own informal leader. In any case, these groups form for the purpose of assisting senators in getting support for legislation which is important to them by arranging vote trades on different bills.

In the voting model expected by this behavioral coalition explanation, the constituency coefficients should be important, indicating that senators give some weight on a consistent basis to their constituents. The formal and informal leaders should also have significant coefficients in many legislators' equations, indicating membership in a party or subparty coalition. The magnitudes and significances of these leaders' coefficients should exhibit definite patterns among legislators depending upon the subparty coalition in which each legislator is active.

The substantial influence of both constituencies and the various formal and informal leaders is consistent with this description. The concentration of the significant coefficients for Mansfield, Humphrey, the committee chairman, and the committee liberal variables among separate blocs within the Democratic party indicates the existence of several subcoalitions within the party. The existence of these formally and informally organized coalitions also solves part of the problem which organizational theorists use as the basis for their limited information models. Once senators join an existing coalition, whether it is the formal party, the group of more liberal eastern Democrats, or the conservative Republicans, they can concentrate on the legislation important to them and rely on someone else for cues on how to vote. This reduces the information and time constraint problems which Matthews and Stimpson emphasize.

There is one last result which is useful in evaluating the legislative behavior models and which is consistent with the pure coalition explanation. The statistical models tested here have much poorer fits for the group of senators identified as western Democrats. These are Democrats from the Rocky Mountain, southwestern, and Pacific states. The estimated equations explain more than half of the variance in the voting behavior of only 9 of these 23 senators, while the fits of 63 of the remaining 78 senators exceed this level. It is hypothesized that these senators have a higher propensity to trade their votes on most bills for other considerations, such as support on a public power bill or other legislation favorable to mountain and western states or for future committee assignments, such as interior or public works. Several people mentioned that on most bills, it was easier to bargain with senators in this western group than most other senators. A former aide to Lyndon Johnson, when he was the majority leader, said, "Thank goodness there was a group of senators like the western Democrats. You could always count on getting a vote or two from them if you needed it."[17] These comments strongly suggest that vote trades or special pleas from party leaders played a more important role in the voting of western Democrats than for other senators. These considerations are excluded from the formal part of the model in Eqs. 2.1 and 2.2 and are included in the error term, e. This reduces the explanatory power of the models and results in lower R^2's, as observed. The vote trading explanation is quite consistent with the coalition approach to legislative behavior, while the leadership plea notion is consistent with the traditional formal leadership view. An examination of the voting behavior on the individual bills in Chapter 6 will be used to try to further discriminate between these alternative explanations.

APPENDIX 4.1. DISTRIBUTION OF COEFFICIENTS IN FULL EQUATIONS

Group	Number of senators with coefficients in each range							
	≤ -0.25	-0.15 -0.24	-0.14 0.14	0.15 0.24	0.25 0.49	0.50 0.74	0.75 0.99	≥ 1.00
A. Constituency								
E. Dem.	—	—	4	4	9	2	3	1
S. Dem.	—	—	—	1	1	2	5	9
W. Dem.	—	1	2	1	9	7	1	2
E. Rep.	—	—	2	—	1	4	4	7
W. Rep.	1	—	1	2	2	2	7	4
B. Party leaders								
E. Dem.								
Mansfield	2	2	10	6	2	—	1	—
Humphrey	5	1	7	1	3	2	3	—
S. Dem.								
Mansfield	2	1	12	2	1	—	—	—
Humphrey	1	3	9	3	2	—	—	—
W. Dem.								
Mansfield	—	—	12	2	7	1	—	—
Humphrey	3	3	9	3	3	1	—	—

APPENDIX 4.1. DISTRIBUTION OF COEFFICIENTS IN FULL EQUATIONS

Group	Number of senators with coefficients in each range							
	≤-0.25	-0.15 -0.24	-0.14 0.14	0.15 0.24	0.25 0.49	0.50 0.74	0.75 0.99	≥1.00
E. Rep.								
Dirksen	1	4	8	–	4	1	–	–
Kuchel	–	1	14	3	–	–	–	–
Pol.	–	–	–	–	–	–	–	–
Com.[a]	2	3	8	1	2	–	–	–
W. Rep.								
Dirksen	1	–	13	2	2	–	–	–
Kuchel	1	–	15	1	–	–	–	–
Pol.	–	–	–	–	–	–	–	–
Com.[a]	4	1	10	1	1	–	–	–
C. Committe leaders								
E. Dem.								
Chairman	1	3	17	2	–	–	–	–
Liberal	3	–	5	–	4	2	2	2
S. Dem.								
Chairman	–	2	11	3	2	–	–	–
Russell	4	4	5	3	1	–	–	–

91

W. Dem.								
Chairman	—	1	14	7	1	—	1	—
Liberal	—	—	3	2	2	2	1	—
E. Rep.								
Minority	—	—	—	—	—	—	—	—
Leader	—	2	13	3	—	—	—	—
Conservative	—	—	1	—	2	—	2	—
W. Rep.								
Minority	—	—	—	—	—	—	—	—
Leader	—	1	13	4	1	—	1	2
Conservative	—	1	4	—	2	2	2	2
D. President								
E. Dem.	—	1	15	4	3	—	—	—
S. Dem.	2	2	12	1	1	—	—	—
W. Dem.	—	3	15	4	1	—	—	—
E. Rep.	—	4	10	1	2	—	—	—
W. Rep.	1	2	14	—	—	—	—	—

[a]Coefficients for the Republican Policy Committee.

[5] Estimates of 1963 Voting Behavior: A Test of the Models

The statistical models presented here can also be evaluated in terms of their ability to explain behavior subsequent to that used in the statistical analysis. In the case of senate voting, the senators' equations discussed in the previous chapters are used to predict votes cast during the 1963 session. The models discussed in Chapter 4 are evaluated on the basis of their ability to predict the 1963 behavior. The evaluation is done in two steps. The first is simply to ascertain how well the estimated equations fit the senators' 1963 scale scores. Good fits for a large number of senators should provide additional assurances that the estimated equations represent the systematic aspects of senators' voting behavior. The second step focuses on the senators whose votes are not predicted well by the estimated models. If the poor fits result from a few predictable systematic changes in the weight certain senators gave to specific influences, there is less reason to doubt the basic model. The changes indicate simply that some senators changed their behavior in a predictable fashion. At the same time, any systematic changes may provide more information with which to evaluate the different explanations of legislative voting. For example, if constituency is more important as the

time for reelection approaches and if it is less important immediately after a reelection, it would provide additional support
for a representational explanation.

EXPLAINING 1963 VOTING

The votes used in this evaluation process were those cast on
twenty-five items considered by the senate prior to President
Kennedy's assassination in 1963. The bills, votes, and subsequent
scales were shown in Table 3.1. The 1963 session of the senate
is particularly appropriate as a test. It follows the years used to
estimate the models, and there was very little change in the
membership and virtually no change in the leadership positions.
Only fourteen senators did not return for the fall term, and one
of these, Kefauver (D., Tenn.), was alive for votes on nine of
the twenty-five bills. Thus, 86 senators' votes could be predicted
on the first nine bills, and 83 senators' votes on the remainder.[1]

The Variables

In making these predictions, the first steps are to determine
the president's position on each bill and to construct a constituency variable for each senator. The remaining variables in the
models, such as the majority leader and the appropriate committee member variables, are contained in the scales themselves.
The presidential and constituency variables are constructed in the
same fashion as the variables for estimating the equations, which
were discussed in Chapter 3. The presidential variables were
simply President Kennedy's position on the twenty-five Guttman
scales, and a dummy variable for the bills where the *Congressional
Quarterly* reported no position. The constituency variables are
estimated with the same constituency characteristics and by the
same procedure described in Chapter 3 and in Appendix A. This
means the senators' predicted 1963 scale scores are not true
predictions in the usual sense of the word because their actual
votes are required to obtain the constituency variables. However,
the estimated votes are predictions in the sense that the equations

are not reestimated, and senators are assumed to give the same weight to their constituencies and to their leaders as was estimated with the 1961–62 data.

Senators' 1963 voting scales are predicted using the equations estimated for them and the values of the variables included in their equations.[2] These predicted scale scores are then compared with the actual scale scores to ascertain how well these models could explain this additional data.

The Measures of the Equations' Explanatory Powers

Two different measures are used to evaluate these equations. Both are based on the prediction errors, which are the differences between the predicted and the actual scale scores. The first measure is analogous to the R^2 statistic traditionally used to evaluate statistical models. The traditional R^2 is a comparison of the sum of squared errors in the regression equation to the variance of the dependent variable. In the case of the prediction equations, the comparison is between the sum of the squared prediction errors and the variance of the senators' 1963 scale scores. Rather than calling this comparison an R^2, it will be referred to as the $(1-U^2)$ statistic.[3] The second measure is a comparison of the square root of the sum of the squared errors from the 1963 data with the estimated standard deviations of the errors in the 1961–62 equations presented in Chapter 4. (The first term in this comparison would be the standard deviation of the prediction errors if the errors had a zero mean.) The difference between these two standard deviations is referred to as (RMSE–SE).[4]

As is the case with R^2 values, the $(1-U^2)$ statistic has an upper bound of one, indicating that the equation is predicting perfectly and that there are no prediction errors. A value of $(1-U^2)$ between one and zero is analogous to an R^2 and compares the prediction errors to the variance of the variable being predicted. Contrary to the R^2, the $(1-U^2)$ has no lower bound. A value of zero indicates that the sum of squared prediction errors equals the variance of the observed scale scores, and negative $(1-U^2)$ values indicate that the sum of the prediction errors squared is larger than the variance of the scale scores being predicted. The (RMSE–SE) statistic compares the prediction errors from the 1963 observations to the residuals from the analysis of the senators' 1961–62 votes. In essence, this second measure is comparing the equations' 1963 performance with their ability to explain the 1961–62 votes. One statistic, the $(1-U^2)$, is an absolute measure of the equations' explanatory power, while the other, the (RMSE–SE), is a relative measure. Senators could have low $(1-U^2)$ values, indicating that the equations are not explaining much of their voting behavior, yet have small (RMSE–SE) values if the equations do not have a good fit on the data used to estimate the equation. In this case, one would conclude that the equations' prediction performances are as good as could be expected, given their original inability to account for the senators' votes.

The distribution of $(1-U^2)$ values is shown in Table 5.1. These values indicate that the variances of the prediction errors are substantially less than the variances in senators' 1963 scale scores. Forty-four of the senators (51.2 percent) had $(1-U^2)$ values greater than 0.50 and 11 of 86 (less than 15 percent) had negative $(1-U^2)$ values. This means that on something similar to an R^2 basis, the estimated equations are explaining over 50 percent of the variance in the scale scores of half the senators. The distribu-

TABLE 5.1. DISTRIBUTION OF $(1-U^2)$ VALUES FOR INDIVIDUAL SENATORS

Group	< 0.00	0.00 0.24	0.25 0.49	0.50 0.74	0.75 0.99	Total
E. Dem.	4	4	2	7	4	21
S. Dem.	0	0	4	11	3	18
W. Dem.	5	4	3	4	2	18
E. Rep.	0	2	4	8	0	14
W. Rep.	2	3	5	5	0	15
Total	11	13	18	35	9	86

tion of the $(1-U^2)$ values by geographic and party grouping parallels the distribution of R^2 values for the fitted models (see Table 4.1). The fits for the 1963 votes are best for southern Democrats, about equal for Republicans and eastern Democrats and poorest for both western Democrats and western Republicans. The only difference is that for the 1961–62 votes the fits for the western Republicans are equivalent to those for eastern Republicans.

Most of the evaluation will be on the basis of the differences between the equations' ability to explain the 1961–62 votes and their predictions in 1963 as denoted by the (RMSE–SE) values. Large values for this statistic identify the senators whose 1963 votes are not described well by the model that best fit their 1961–62 behavior and who are suspected of changing their behavior. Hopefully the behavior changes of these senators can be related to a few systematic explanations.

The (RMSE–SE) differences are shown in Table 5.2. About half (52 percent) of the values are less than 0.10 and less than a third (31 percent) are greater than 0.24. If a similar comparison is made using the ratio RMSE/SE, which measures the percentage difference rather than the absolute difference in the two values, half the values are less than 1.12 and only twenty-six senators have ratios larger than 1.33. Thus, most senators have 1963

TABLE 5.2. DISTRIBUTION OF 1963 ROOT MEAN SQUARED ERRORS MINUS STANDARD ERRORS FROM 1961–62 REGRESSIONS

Group	< 0.00	0.00 0.09	0.10 0.24	0.25 0.49	⩾ 0.50
E. Dem.	6	4	2	4	5
S. Dem.	7	7	2	1	1
W. Dem.	5	6	2	4	1
E. Rep.	3	3	5	3	0
W. Rep.	0	3	4	5	3
Total	21	23	15	17	10

errors with an estimated standard deviation (assuming a zero mean error) which is within 12 percent of the estimated standard deviation of the 1961–62 errors, and only twenty-six are more than 33 percent greater than their 1961–62 values. The senators who fall outside the 33 percent range are the ones with the greatest differences in Table 5.2. Using either criteria then, a majority of the fits for the 1963 voting are close to the expected fits, where the expected fit is based on the models' ability to explain the 1961–62 voting behavior. The distributions of the (RMSE–SE) differences and of the $(1-U^2)$ values suggest that the models and the estimated importance of the various influences outlined in Chapter 2 do represent the systematic aspects of senatorial voting behavior.

THE MODEL FAILURES

Some senators' 1963 votes deviated substantially from those predicted by the individual equations. Determining why the models failed in these deviant cases should provide further insight into senators' voting behavior if the failures represent systematic shifts in the importance of different influences. The objective is to use the alternative explanations of legislative decision-making to predict the shifts likely to account for the failures. Further support for one of the explanations will be provided if the anticipated shifts are observed. If the cases of model failure are attributable to systematic shifts, it will also substantiate the claims that there is a large systematic component to senators' voting behavior and that the models described in Chapter 2 captured this systematic behavior. The trick will be to specify beforehand precisely which shifts are likely to occur for each senator whose equation failed.

Three shifts are considered possible explanations for the models' failures. The first is in senators' responsiveness to their constituents. It is anticipated that senators give less weight to their constituency immediately following an election, and that constituency influences increase preceding an election. Senators reelected in 1962 should have lower constituency coefficients in 1963 while the remaining senators' constituency coefficients should remain the same or increase, particularly in the case of those up for reelection in 1964. At the same time, changes in the influence of the leaders should follow the opposite pattern. Senators reelected in 1962 and exhibiting smaller constituency influence should show increased responsiveness to the organizational influences. Conversely, the senators who increase the weight they give their constituencies because they are closer to an election should have smaller organizational influences.[5] The basis for these predicted influence changes is the representational model presented by MacRae.[6] He contends that the larger the impact of a vote on a legislator's probability of reelection, the greater the consideration given to the constituency's position. In the case of senators, with their six-year terms, the effect of floor votes on the chances for reelection are likely to increase during the term, with votes cast in the last session being more important than votes cast five or six years previously. This representational explanation expects the influence of constituency to increase during senators' terms in office and then to drop immediately following reelection.

Another expected change is the influence of the president. Many writers have commented upon the frustration President Kennedy experienced with Congress in 1963.[7] This suggests that some senators were voting against his preferences, although much of the frustration concerned legislation which the committees prevented from getting to the floor. There were also some senate liberals who felt that President Kennedy was not pushing liberal legislation, particularly civil rights, hard enough. These senators tried to push some of these positions themselves in spite of the president's position.[8] The observations suggest that some senators were possibly voting in opposition to the president and that the presidential influence observed among northern Democrats in 1961–62 may not have carried into 1963.

The last change anticipated is among senators who were fresh-

men in 1961–62. The results imply that many freshmen senators
give considerable weight to the positions of their senior partner
if both are from the same party. The expectation is for this
weight to decrease as the new senators get acclimated, find their
own cue sources, make their own coalition agreements, and so
forth. The weight the junior senators give to their party leaders
and constituencies should increase as the influence of the senior
partner decreases.

The expectations about changes in senators' behavior are
examined by estimating the importance of each influence on the
1963 votes cast by the senators whose equations failed. The
estimated 1963 coefficients are then compared with the coefficients in the 1961–62 equation.[9] The differences in the importance
of each influence are obtained in such a way that the conventional
statistical tests can be performed on the estimated differences.
Thus, if a difference is statistically significant, one could conclude
that the influences on the senators' decisions had changed.

Definitions of model failures and the selection of senators to
be reanalyzed are based on the cases where the prediction errors
are substantially larger than the errors obtained in estimating the
equations. With four exceptions, the senators in Table 5.2 with
(RMSE–SE) values greater than 0.09 are reexamined. This list
corresponds to the group of senators whose RMSE/SE ratios
exceed 1.15. Table 5.3 lists the senators, their reelection year,
the $(1-U^2)$ value for the predicted votes, and the (RMSE-SE)
differences. The excluded senators are Gore, whose senior senator
died early in the year, and Dodd, Smith (Me.), and Kuchel,
whose RMSE/SE ratios are less than 1.15.

Coefficient Changes

The significant changes in the constituency coefficients are
shown in Table 5.4. Over half the senators examined showed
measurable changes in the influence they accorded their constituents. Only three senators deviated from the pattern of the
anticipated changes. Javits (R., N.Y.), Bennett (R., Utah) and

TABLE 5.3. SENATORS SELECTED FOR 1963 REESTIMATION

	1962			1964			1966		
Senator	RMSE -S.E.	$(1-U^2)$	Senator	RMSE -S.E.	$(1-U^2)$	Senator	RMSE -S.E.	$(1-U^2)$
Lausche	0.77	-0.46	Young	0.64	-0.33	Miller[a]	0.67	-0.11
Hickenlooper	0.52	0.38	Burdick	0.55	-0.12	Randolph	0.66	-0.01
Morse	0.49	-0.01	Proxmire	0.52	0.25	McClellan	0.55	0.29
Javits	0.48	0.17	Fong	0.49	-0.45	Anderson	0.50	-0.84
Young (N.D.)	0.47	0.54	Symington	0.37	0.21	Tower[a]	0.50	0.10
Hayden	0.35	0.24	Beall	0.25	0.24	Pell[a]	0.31	0.59
Clark	0.29	0.23	Keating	0.22	0.52	Thurmond	0.31	0.42
Magnuson	0.28	-0.65	Prouty	0.12	0.57	Curtis	0.30	0.15
Dirksen	0.28	0.30				Douglas	0.30	0.23
Cotton	0.27	0.57				Neuberger	0.28	0.08
Bennett	0.23	0.07				Allott	0.25	0.36
Monroney	0.23	0.14				Case (N.J.)[a]	0.23	0.45
Gruening	0.16	0.60				Pearson[a]	0.19	0.62
Ervin	0.13	0.71				Mundt	0.19	0.60
						Eastland	0.19	0.68
						Boggs[a]	0.15	0.67

[a]Freshman in 1961-62

100

TABLE 5.4. CHANGES IN THE CONSTITUENCY COEFFICIENTS

Direction of change	Reelection year		
	1962	1964	1966
None[a]	7	4	7
Negative[b]	4	0	0
Positive[b]	3	4	9

[a]Change coefficient not significant at the 5% level.
[b]Change coefficient significant at the 5% level.

Morse (D., Oreg.), all reelected in 1962, showed higher constituency effects. The remaining senators exhibited the expected changes, those reelected in 1962 giving the same or less weight to their constituents in 1963, while those facing reelection in 1964 or 1966 gave them at least as much weight as previously.

The changes in the influence of the party leaders and committee members are the opposite of the changes in the constituency influences. The senators who gave more weight to their constituents in 1963 than in 1961 and 1962 gave less weight to the internal sources, and those who gave less weight to their constituents in 1963 than previously gave more weight to the internal sources. There are ten statistically significant changes in leadership coefficients among the group of senators reelected in 1962, and five of these are negative. Three of the cases of decreased leadership influence, however, were the senators who increased their constituency's influence. In the group of eight senators facing reelection in 1964, there are seven statistically significant changes among the internal influences and only one of these is positive. Thus, the behavior of these senators is consistent with the contention that senators give more weight to their constituencies and less weight to party leaders during the session prior to an election.

The presidential coefficients show that President Kennedy's influence generally declined from 1961–62 to 1963. These changes

are shown in Table 5.5. A third of the senators changed the
weight they gave the president, and only four of them accorded
him greater influence. They were Dirksen (R., Ill.), Eastland
(D., Miss.), Gruening (D., Alaska), and Fong (R., Hawaii). In the
cases of Eastland, Gruening, and Fong, this change means that
in 1963 they did not give any weight to the president's position
whereas in 1961–62 they voted in opposition to him. Dirksen, on
the other hand, gave no weight to the president's positions in
1961 and 1962 (if any relationship did exist, it was a negative
one), but this changed in 1963, with the president having a considerable influence on Dirksen's votes (the coefficient was 0.40).

The negative shifts, indicating reduced presidential influence,
are concentrated among senators up for reelection in 1964 and
1966 and among the more liberal wing of the Democratic party.
The senators in this group are Douglas, Proxmire, Young (Ohio),
and Pell. The remaining senators with negative changes are Clark,
Anderson, and Republicans Case (N.J.), Prouty, and Boggs.
Proxmire, Pell, and Boggs are the only ones among the senators
showing decreased presidential influence who were not directly
and positively influenced by the president in 1961–62. The other
six are virtually all the senators with significant presidential coefficients in 1961–62 who returned in 1963. Thus, either because
of senators not returning or because of altered voting behavior,
by 1963 the president lost all the influence attributed to him in

TABLE 5.5. CHANGES IN THE PRESIDENTIAL COEFFICIENTS

| Direction | Reelection year | | |
of change	1962	1964	1966
None[a]	11	4	10
Negative[b]	1	3	5
Positive[b]	2	1	1

[a]Change coefficient not significant at the 5% level.
[b]Change coefficient significant at the 5% level.

the previous session except for the change in Dirksen's behavior.

The final expected change is the influence freshman senators accorded their senior partner if both are in the same party. All the changes in senior senators' influence are shown in Table 5.6. Five freshmen are included in the group of reestimated equations. Of these, only Tower, whose senior senator was in the other party, was not influenced by his senior colleague in 1961–62. Two of the senators, Miller and Pearson, gave substantially less weight to their senior partner in 1963 than they had in the previous Congress. All five senators significantly increased the importance of their constituency's influence in 1963. Thus, the votes of these senators exhibit considerable constituency influence in 1963, whereas only one, Boggs (R., Del.), had been so influenced in 1961–62.

The two senior senator changes among nonfreshmen were senators running for reelection in 1964, Keating (R., N.Y.) and Prouty (R., Vt.). Keating gave more weight to the positions taken by Javits, his senior partner who had just been reelected, and did not change the influence previously held by his constituents, which had been significantly positive in the previous two years. Prouty both reduced the weight given to his senior partner, Senator Aiken, and increased the influence held by his constituents.

The changes in the influence of the constituency, presidential, and senior senator variables discussed here affects the models of

TABLE 5.6. CHANGES IN THE SENIOR SENATOR COEFFICIENTS

Direction of change	Reelection year		
	1962	1964	1966
None[a]	14(13)[b]	6(6)[b]	14(13)[b]
Negative[c]	0	1	2
Positive[c]	0	1	0

[a]Change coefficient not significant at the 5% level.
[b]Number with coefficient not significant in the 1961–62 model.
[c]Change coefficient significant at the 5% level.

twenty-seven of the senators singled out for examination in Table 5.3. These changes improve the explanatory power of the equations sufficiently to make most compatible with the results of the 1961–62 estimations. The remaining eleven senators fall into three groups. In the cases of seven senators, none of the variables focused on here received different emphasis, but one of the included leadership influences changed. For example, Hayden (D., Ariz.) gave more weight to Mansfield's positions after his reelection in 1962, and Beall (R., Md.) gave less weight to Dirksen prior to his upcoming campaign in 1964. In the cases of three others, Young (N.D.), Cotton, and Mundt, the variables which were significant in 1961–62 have virtually the same influence in 1963, but these influences explain fewer of the senators' votes than previously. These senators, two of whom were reelected in 1962, have large constituency coefficients during all three years. The reestimated equations indicate that they gave the same weight to their constituents in 1963 as in 1961–62 but were more likely to deviate from these positions on a nonsystematic basis. The remaining senator was Neuberger. The model had not been able to explain her voting behavior in 1961–62, and no influences are significant in either 1961–62 or in 1963.

The changes in one senator's decisions are worthy of special attention and some brief speculation. This is the case of Senator Dirksen, the Republican floor leader. In the session prior to his reelection in 1962, Dirksen's votes were largely determined by his constituency's positions, with some weight given to the positions taken by the ranking Republican and a conservative member of the reporting committee. In 1963, however, his constituency coefficient fell from 1.01 to 0.42, while the coefficient on the president's positions rose from a small negative number to over 0.40. Thus, Dirksen moved from being quite constituency oriented prior to the election to being supportive of the president.

If this relationship between Dirksen and Kennedy is not spurious, it indicates some form of agreement between the two. The interesting speculation is whether Dirksen's floor votes were reflecting President Kennedy's positions in exchange for presidential consideration of things important to Dirksen, or whether Dirksen was influencing the president's positions on legislation before the whole Senate in exchange for assistance from Dirksen and other Republicans in getting President Kennedy's bills through the committees. The fact that Dirksen's constituency coefficient decreased significantly indicates that he substantially changed his floor voting behavior, so it is likely that Dirksen's floor votes were being influenced by the president's positions. If the reverse effect were true and the president was adopting Dirksen's positions, there would have been no reason for the other coefficients in Dirksen's equation to change.

If Dirksen's support of the president resulted from a conscious arrangement made by President Kennedy, anticipating that Dirksen's support would mean Republican votes on the floor of the senate, it appears to have been a poor bargain. The results of the models estimated for 1961–62 indicate that Dirksen had only limited systematic influence over members of his own party when it came to floor votes. Dirksen had significant positive coefficients in the models of only seven fellow Republicans. His influence was further diminished according to the 1963 estimations, which suggest that three of the previously positive coefficients changed signs, and one positive coefficient went to zero. The changes are Fong (0.48 to −0.25), Beall (0.24 to −0.12), and Miller (0.34 to −0.11). Allott's coefficient for Dirksen's position went from 0.34 to 0.04. However, his change of −0.30 is not statistically significant. In addition, two Republican senators who exhibited no Dirksen influence in 1961–62 have significant negative coefficients for him in 1963, while only one senator went from a zero to a positive coefficient during the period. The net effect of these changes means that Dirksen positively influenced very few senators on a systematic basis. Consequently, getting Dirksen's votes did not bring along a lot of additional support on floor votes. At the same time, Kennedy appears to have lost the support of several of the more liberal members of his own party. This is indicated by the negative coefficients for the 1963 presidential variable for senators Douglas, Clark, Proxmire, Young, and Pell. As interesting as it might be, establishing any sort of association between these two observations, for example, that Kennedy's effort to gain Dirksen's support alienated the more liberal members of his own party, would be difficult to establish.

PREDICTIONS AND MODELS OF SENATE VOTING BEHAVIOR

The analysis of senators' 1963 votes has provided several useful pieces of information about the models of Senate voting behavior. The fact that the equations discussed in Chapter 4 explain a substantial portion of the 1963 voting behavior of most senators suggests that there is a large systematic component to their voting decisions and that these simple equations capture this systematic behavior. Consequently, any observations drawn from the results presented in Chapter 4 about the applicability of the different explanations of legislative behavior would appear to have some validity.

The reestimation of the voting models for the senators whose 1963 votes were not predicted well by their 1961–62 equations further supports the contention that the basic models represent systematic aspects of senators' voting. In the first place, for most of the thirty-eight senators examined, 1963 voting behavior is explained as well as 1961–62 behavior once the weights given the influences in each equation are adjusted. Secondly, over two-thirds of the adjustments made to obtain the improved explanatory ability are consistent with at least one of the three changes in influence predicted at the beginning of the analysis. The fact that the equations fit the 1963 votes as well as they do the 1961–62 votes once the coefficients on the variables already in the equations are adjusted implies that the equations are specified properly. The additional fact that the most frequent change, namely the shifts in the constituency coefficients, is predicted by one of the representational explanations of legislative behavior, and that most of the other changes are consistent with reported political circumstances (in this case the decline of presidential influence) gives further credence both to the estimated equations and to the representational explanation of legislative behavior from which the predicted change is derived.

The examination of the shifts in senators' voting behavior strongly supports the type of representational model proposed by MacRae. According to MacRae's model, the greater the effect of a roll call vote on the probability of reelection, the more likely the legislators are to vote with their constituents. If one accepts the proposition that votes cast closer to senators' reelection campaigns have more impact on their chances for reelection, then, according to MacRae, senators will exhibit more constituency influence closer to an election.

[6] Voting Behavior on Specific Legislation

The final part of this study looks at the ability of the models to explain the voting behavior observed on the individual items of legislation. There are several questions which can be discussed in this way. Just in terms of substantive interest, many people are proponents of particular legislative items and are more interested in voting behavior on individual bills than in the voting decisions of individual senators. This chapter should satisfy their curiosity about the fit of these models to the specific bills used in the study and listed in Chapter 3. The analysis of the voting behavior on individual bills also permits a comparison of the models estimated here with the more traditional studies which have compared senators' votes on a particular bill or issue index with constituency and party variables. More importantly, this analysis should provide a further evaluation of the different explanations of legislative behavior. The alternative explanations for legislative roll call voting behavior are expected to differ in their ability to explain senators' positions on various issues. This chapter will compare the equations' performance on each bill and hopefully contribute to the evaluation of the models by ascertaining what pattern, if any, exists to the models' performance.

THE OVERALL PERFORMANCE OF THE MODELS

The first comparisons are between the explanatory ability of the models discussed in Chapter 4 and alternative ways of predicting the voting behavior observed on each bill. Comparisons with the alternatives will provide yardsticks for evaluating the performance of the estimated individual equations. The performance measure used to make the comparisons is the same $(1-U^2)$ statistic used in Chapter 5.[1] Only now the sum of the squared prediction errors from the individual equations will be compared to the sum of the prediction errors from the alternative predictions.

The first alternative model is simply the mean score of all the senators voting on each bill. Again it should be noted that the $(1-U^2)$ for this model is comparable to the conventional R^2 value for a regression model. Although the mean scale score is an absurdly naïve model, it is being used because of the similarity its $(1-U^2)$ value has to the R^2 statistic which is widely used to evaluate regression models. The $(1-U^2)$ statistics from comparisons with this model will be called $[1-U^2 \text{ (MEAN)}]$.

The second and more plausible naïve model is obtained by regressing the scale scores of the senators voting on a bill against the values of their constituency variable for that bill and their party. This model is shown as Equation 6.1.

$$(6.1) \qquad V = b_0 + b_1 \text{ Constituency} + b_2 \text{ Party} + e$$

where V is the vote of each senator; Constituency is the position of senators' constituencies; and Party is the party of each senator.

The party variable in Eq. 6.1 is measured as 1 for Republicans and 0 for Democrats. This variable summarizes the leadership effects included separately in the previous individual equations. The party leaders' positions cannot be included as separate explanatory variables in Eq. 6.1 because the equation is being estimated separately for each bill. A party floor leader variable has the same value for all Republicans and the same value for all

Democrats, as would party whip and committee leader variables, making them no different than the party dummy variable. The total party related influences then are summarized in the party dummy variable. The $(1-U^2)$ statistic for comparisons with this constituency and party model are labelled $[1-U^2 \ (\text{BILL})]$.

The model presented in Eq. 6.1 is similar to most previous attempts to examine legislative voting behavior, as is the fact that it is estimated for individual bills, using senators as separate observations.[2] Most studies have tried to correlate voting on specific bills with party and constituency variables. There is one major difference in the assumptions made by the model in Eq. 6.1 and the assumptions of the individual models discussed in Chapter 4. The alternative party and constituency model implies that on each bill all senators give the same weight to constituency preferences and to the positions of their party leaders, namely b_1 and b_2 respectively. Since the equation is estimated separately for each bill, the further implication is that the influences of constituencies and leaders, although the same for all senators, is permitted to vary for different bills. For example, the constituency influence, b_1, is the same for all senators but will be different for each bill. The equations discussed in Chapter 4 make alternative assumptions. The individual senators' equations permit considerable variation in the weight individual senators give to their constituencies and their party leaders, as evidenced by the distributions presented in the tables. However, the individual models imply that the weights the individual senators give their constituency and their party leaders do not vary among different bills but are the same regardless of whether the senate is voting on civil rights or on amendments to the Sugar Quota Act. The $[1-U^2 \ (\text{BILL})]$ statistic constitutes an evaluation of each assumption based on how well the models embodying each assumption fit the observed voting data. The higher the value of $[1-U^2 \ (\text{BILL})]$, the better the models allowing variation among individual senators do relative to the models permitting influence variation across different bills.

The comparisons of the individual models with the party and constituency model is done only for the 1961–62 bills. Because the votes estimated for 1963 are predictions based on the individual 1961–62 equations, it is not clear what predictions would be comparable using the 1961–62 constituency and party equations. If it were possible to find completely analogous bills in both sessions, then it would be appropriate to use the coefficients estimated for the 1961–62 constituency and party equation to predict the 1963 votes and to compare these predictions with those of the individual equations discussed in Chapter 5. Because it would require heroic assumptions to associate each 1963 bill with one of the earlier bills, it was decided to omit this part of the analysis and to compare the party and constituency models only with the individual equations for 1961–62.

The 1961–62 Bills

The distributions of the $(1-U^2)$ values for each alternative model in 1961–62 are presented in Table 6.1. The distribution of the $(1-U^2)$ values indicates that the predictions based on the individual models are definitely superior in all cases to predictions based on the mean scale score and are superior, but not by so large a margin, to predictions based only on constituency and party. For the naïve model based on the mean, nearly half the bills have $(1-U^2)$ values greater than 0.80, which corresponds to an R^2 value greater than 0.80. Only one bill, Amendments to the Sugar Quota Act, has a $(1-U^2)$ value less than 0.60. These ratios imply that on a mean squared error criteria, the individual models explain the scale scores at least twice as well as the mean on all but one bill, and five times as well on sixteen of the thirty-six bills.

When the errors of the individual models are compared to the errors from the simple constituency and party-model, twenty had $(1-U^2)$ values greater than 0.50, meaning that on 55 percent of the bills, the individual models have less than half the mean squared error of the constituency and party model. Thus, models which postulate different decision models for each senator

TABLE 6.1. DISTRIBUTION OF $(1-U^2)$ STATISTICS

Naïve model	Number of bills with $(1-U^2)$ statistics in each range								
	0.00–0.19	0.20–0.29	0.30–0.39	0.40–0.49	0.50–0.59	0.60–0.69	0.70–0.79	0.80–0.99
Mean score	–	–	1	–	–	4	15	16
Constituency and party	2	4	3	7	10	9	1	–

but constrain each model to be the same for all bills perform better than models which permit the influence of different factors to vary with each bill but constrain each senator to have the same set of weights for these factors.

The bills with $[1-U^2$ (BILL)] values less than 0.40 are shown in Table 6.2. There appear to be two types of bills for which the individual models do not do significantly better than the simple constituency and party model. Of the nine bills with $[1-U^2$ (BILL)] values less than 0.40, four are civil rights bills, four are pork barrel or local interest issues (sugar amendments, public works, maritime subsidy, and the national wilderness), and the other is the amendments to the Agriculture Act of 1961 (trying

TABLE 6.2. BILLS WITH $[1-U^2$ (BILL)] VALUES LESS THAN 0.40

Bill	$[1-U^2$ (BILL)] [a]	Rank[a]	$[1-U^2$ (MEAN)] [b]	Rank[b]
Civil Rights Commission (1961-13)	0.05	36	0.85	7
Sugar Act (1962-10)	0.11	35	0.39	36
Agriculture Act of 1961 (1961-8)	0.24	34	0.64	32
Poll Taxes (1962-2)	0.26	33	0.76	26
Literacy Tests (1962-4)	0.29	32	0.79	17
Omnibus Public Works (1961-18)	0.29	31	0.66	33
Maritime Subsidy (1962-18)	0.36	30	0.62	34
D.C. Voting Rights (1961-17)	0.36	29	0.76	27
National Wilderness (1961-14)	0.39	28	0.61	35

[a] $(1-U^2)$ values and ranks for comparing individual models with the bill models based on constituency and party.

[b] $(1-U^2)$ values and ranks for comparing individual models with the mean scale score on each bill.

to limit farm cooperative mergers), which also might be considered more of a local interest bill.

The four civil rights bills have very large and significant coefficients for the constituency variable and negligible coefficients for the party variable in the party and constituency model. Both the individual senators' equations and the constituency and party models explain a high percentage of the variance in the voting behavior on these bills.

The remaining bills for which the differences in the explanatory power of the two models are small are those for which neither model predicts the voting well. These five bills all have relatively low values for the $[1-U^2$ (MEAN)$]$ statistic. Since this is analogous to a ranking by an explained variance criteria, the $[1-U^2$ (MEAN)$]$ values indicate that the individual models do not account for as much of the variance in voting behavior on these bills as on the other bills.

There are interesting similarities among the five bills with the lowest $[1-U^2$ (MEAN)$]$ values. They all evoke strong images of local interests, pork barrel legislation, and the accompanying vote trading and logrolling. The increased importance or presence of these factors decreases the explanatory power both of the individual models and of the constituency and party equations, since neither includes measures for such effects.

The results in Table 6.2 are also consistent with the behavioral or sophisticated representational explanation of legislative voting. The five bills which are most poorly explained are of a limited interest to most voters in a majority of the states, even though they may be extremely important to groups in some of the states. Thus, they are prime candidates for the type of vote trading expected by the sophisticated representational model. Senators trying to pass or defeat civil rights legislation, Medicare, or school assistance because they are important issues may agree to support or oppose the limited interest bills in exchange for the support of senators from states affected by sugar quotas, maritime subsidies, etc. Evans and Novak in their book on Lyndon B. Johnson recounted an instance where Johnson, as Senate Majority Leader, got a Rocky Mountain Democrat to support the position Johnson was taking on a civil rights bill to avoid a southern filibuster in return for Johnson's support on a bill authorizing a public works and public power project in the Democrat's home state. It was the Rocky Mountain senator's stand on the project which was supposedly significant in helping him defeat the Republican incumbent two years earlier.[3] For this explanation to be valid, the senators interested in civil rights, Medicare, school assistance, and so on must be relatively indifferent about such bills as sugar quotas, maritime subsidies, and public power. The converse must hold for senators interested in the latter bills. They must be relatively indifferent about civil rights, Medicare, or schooling legislation. Both of these requirements are quite likely true in the previous examples.

This explanation for the five bills with the poorest fits is also consistent with observed overall fits for the models of the western Democrats. The individual equations have by far their worst fits for these senators (see Table 4.1). It is quite possible that western senators were likely to be relatively indifferent toward more of the legislation considered during this Congress than any other set of senators. At the same time the legislation that was likely important to them, which would surely include some of the five bills under discussion, does not seem to have been central to the senators and constituencies concerned with the civil rights bills, the labor legislation, area redevelopment, or other social and urban programs. Thus, all the requirements seem to be met for the type of vote trading expected by the sophisticated representational model.

The good fits on the four civil rights bills are also very consistent with the representational model. It was pointed out earlier, and also by Miller and Stokes in their work on a pure constituency model, that civil rights was probably the single most salient issue in many constituencies. It undoubtedly was the most important issue among sizable and significant voting blocs in many senators' states. Senators certainly endangered their careers if they ignored the presence of such a highly concerned group of voters, particularly if no opposing group of roughly equal size existed within the voting population which also considered civil rights the most important issue. It seems likely that the general mood toward civil rights in the early 1960's fits this description. In most states outside the South, the groups most concerned with civil rights were strong advocates of it. Just the reverse was true in the South when only the voting populace is considered. Consequently, most senators were likely voting with their constituencies on the civil rights bills. The results show precisely this pattern. The civil rights bills have much higher fits for the equations estimated, or based on, the constituency variables. This result is consistent with the sophisticated representational model and in fact is predicted by this explanation.

1963 Bills

Before examining some of the hypothesized differences in goodness of fit among the five groups of senators, the $[1-U^2$ (MEAN)$]$ statistics are presented for the 1963 bills. Table 6.3 shows the distribution of the $[1-U^2$ (MEAN)$]$ values for the 1963 legislation. On seventeen of the twenty-five bills, the scale scores predicted by the individual models are at least twice as good as the mean scale score on a mean squared error basis. Thus, the conclusion that the estimated models have a reasonable amount of predictive power, also made in Chapter 5, seems justified.

The values for individual bills are more interesting than the

TABLE 6.3. $[1-U^2$ (MEAN)$]$ VALUES FOR THE TWENTY-FIVE BILLS FROM 1963

	Number of bills with $[1-U^2$ (MEAN)$]$ values in each range						
< 0.00	0.00–0.19	0.20–0.29	0.30–0.39	0.40–0.49	0.50–0.59	0.60–0.69	0.70–0.79
2	1	1	—	4	5	6	6

overall distribution of the $(1-U^2)$ values. Table 6.4 lists the bills
with the highest and lowest $[1-U^2 \text{ (MEAN)}]$ values for the 1963
bills. The bills with the highest $(1-U^2)$ values are the Youth
Employment Act, the National Service Corps, the Feed Grains
Acreage Diversion Program, Manpower Training and Development,
Vocational Education, and Water Resources Act. Only the Feed
Grains Acreage and Water Resource program are not similar to the
bills predicted well in the 1961-1962 sample.

The most interesting results here are the bills with the poorest
fits on the criteria equivalent to an R^2. The models performed
quite badly on only four bills—two appropriations bills, a labor
arbitration resolution, and amendments to restrict the president's
control of foreign aid. Both appropriations acts had undercurrents
of local interest, since the votes on both bills dealt with the procurement or development of expensive aerospace products. (The
primary activities being questioned in the independent offices bill
were NASA and the SST.) The strong local economic effects of
such projects, in addition to the strong role of expertise and

TABLE 6.4. BEST AND POOREST FIT 1963 BILLS

Best Fit		Poorest Fit	
Bill	$[1-U^2$ (MEAN)]	Bill	$[1-U^2$ (MEAN)]
Youth Employment Act	0.77	Defense Approp.	−0.27
Feed Grain Acreage	0.76	Indep. Offices Approp.	−0.06
National Service Corps	0.74	Railroad Arbitration	0.11
Manpower Develop.	0.71	Foreign Assistance (Restrictions)	0.21
Vocational Education	0.71	Foreign Assistance (Funding)	0.45
Water Resources	0.70	Committee Sizes and Appropriations	0.46
		Wilderness Preservation	0.47
		Cloture Rule	0.48

authority granted members of the Appropriations Committee, could account for the breakdown of the models on these two bills. The models do not predict much better than the mean on the Railroad Arbitration Resolution because there is virtually no variance in the votes on this bill. (Seventy percent of the scale scores equalled the mean value.) Even though the model only explains a small percentage of the variance on this bill, only three other bills have smaller mean squared errors. A low mean squared error indicates the models are predicting well, even though they may not be explaining much of the variance.

The five scales with $(1-U^2)$ values greater than 0.20 had several interesting characteristics. These are the two scales constructed from the Foreign Assistance Authorization Act, the attempt to change the cloture rule, the organization and funding of senate committees, and the Wilderness Preservation System. With the exception of cloture, the last five poorly fit bills are likely of generally little interest to a majority of the constituents in most states and probably do not affect them directly. Decisions on committee membership and foreign aid would seem to fit this description, for example. The National Wilderness legislation was one of the poorly fit bills in the 1961–62 sample, having the second lowest $(1-U^2)$ value in that group of bills. In situations of limited constituency interest, factors like logrolling, as possibly on the National Wilderness bill, or the influence of important individuals, such as the president or Foreign Relations Committee chairman on the Foreign Assistance Act, will become more important. The increased importance of such factors would result in larger observed deviations from the systematic models.

There is an interesting pattern to the errors on the Defense and Independent Offices Appropriations bills. The errors on both bills are ranked from the largest positive value (predicted value greater than actual) to the largest negative value (predicted less than actual). Positive errors indicate that the senators' observed support for the bill is less than the support predicted by their equations, and vice versa for negative errors. There were six senators (Randolph, Clark, Morse, Ellender, Pell, and Douglas) who have very large positive errors on the Defense Appropriation question. Their residuals range from Douglas's 2.55 to Randolph's 3.76. Five of the six, Ellender excluded, also have large, positive residuals on the Independent Offices Appropriations bill appropriating money for NASA and the SST. In addition, Senators Young (D., Ohio), Neuberger, Burdick, and Fulbright also have positive errors exceeding 1.75 on the Independent Offices bill.

These senators' reluctance to vote for defense and aerospace projects in 1963, coupled with their subsequent stands on the Vietnam war and further aerospace and defense procurement, such as the ABM, seems to be early evidence of the now-apparent liberal position questioning these expenditures. The amendments showed some of this emerging liberal opposition. One amendment offered by Saltonstall to cut defense procurement and research and development appropriations by 1 percent was supported by most conservative Republicans as well as by the liberals, such as Morse and McGovern. An amendment by McGovern to cut this same appropriation by 10 percent was rejected by the Republicans but supported by Democrats like Clark, Morse, and Pell. The amendments trying to reduce NASA and the SST appropriations were offered by Douglas, Proxmire, and Fulbright, again foreshadowing the liberal predisposition against large aerospace appropriations. There is a similar, but not so apparent, indication of things to come among the noted conservatives. For example, Tower is underpredicted by more than 2.00 on both bills, indicating that he voted more in favor of these two appropriations bills, which were likely to help Texas, than his model predicts.

MODEL FITS FOR INDIVIDUAL SENATORS

Additional information about senators' voting behavior is obtained by examining the fits of the equations for the different groups of senators. The comparison of the explanations of legislative behavior in Chapter 2 indicated that each explanation makes different predictions about which bills and for which senators the equations should exhibit their best performance. The example of the coalition model cited earlier suggests that western senators were more likely to trade their votes on civil rights issues to senators determined to pass or defeat such legislation in exchange for support on bills promoting state and regional economic development in the west. The implication here is that the equations should have high fits among southerners on civil rights and among western Democrats on public works and similar bills. Likewise, the equations should exhibit poor fits among southerners on bills favored by western senators and on civil rights for western Democrats. If the coalition model is appropriate, there should be other examples of possible vote trades.

The performance of the estimated equations for the various senators on the different bills is examined by computing separate $[1-U^2 (MEAN)]$ scores for each of the five groups of senators on each bill. The $(1-U^2)$ statistics are computed on the basis of the mean scale score for all senators voting on a bill. The $(1-U^2)$ values computed in this fashion compare the information contained in the individual equations against a no-information model, which says the best guess of a senator's vote on a bill is the mean for all senators.

There are two patterns to watch for among the different comparisons. The first is simply which bills are consistently fit well or poorly for the various senators. For example, it is virtually certain that the civil rights bills will be among the best fit for southern Democrats given the importance of constituency in their models and the importance of civil rights questions to southern voters. It is less obvious which bills should have the best and poorest explanations for the other senators. The second pattern is made by bills that are among the best fit for one group of senators and among the worst fit for a second or third group. Where such a pattern occurs, it suggests that the former group of senators is sticking to their systematic voting behavior while the members of the latter groups are substantially deviating from their systematic patterns. The question then is whether the deviations are the result of logrolling or some other, unaccounted-for influences. The bills which have the best and the poorest fits in each group of senators for each of the two Congresses are shown in Table 6.5.

The bills well fit for each group of senators generally correspond

TABLE 6.5. MODEL FITS FOR SENATE GROUPS

E. Dem.	W. Dem.	S. Dem.
	Best Fits, 1961–1962	
1 Arms Control	College Aid	Civil Rights Comm.
2 School Assist.	Medicare	Literacy Tests
3 Trade Expansion	Manpower	Poll Taxes
4 Minimum Wage	Impacted Areas	Minimum Wage
5 College Aid	School Assistance	D. C. Voting
6 Area Redevelop.	Cultural Exchange	Mexican Farm Labor
7 Manpower	Interior Approp.	Foreign Aid
	Poorest Fits, 1961–1962	
36 Sugar Act	Nat'l Wild.	Maritime
35 Maritime Sub.	Sugar Act	Medicare
34 Agriculture	Poll Tax	Revenue Act
33 Foreign Assist.	Agriculture	Impacted Areas
32 Public Works	Literacy Tests	Sugar Act
31 Nat'l. Wild.	U. N. Bonds	Public Works
30 D. C. Voting	Mexican Farm Labor	Interior Approp.
	Best Fits, 1963	
1 Vocational Ed.	Fishing Vessel	College Aid
2 Manpower	Vocational Ed.	Youth Employ.
3 Nat'l Serv. Corps	Youth Employ.	Cloture Rule
4 Fishing Vessel	Labor-HEW Approp.	Mexican Farm Labor
5 Youth Employ.	Feed Grains	For. Assist.-Funds
	Poorest Fits, 1963	
25 Railroad Labor	Defense App.	Defense App.
24 Defense App.	Mexican Farm Labor	Milk Price Controls
23 Ind. Office App.	Ind. Office App.	Feed Grains
22 For. Assist.-Funds	Railroad Labor	Railroad Labor
21 For. Assist.-Rest.	Cloture Rules	Manpower

TABLE 6.5. (continued)

E. Rep.	W. Rep.
Best Fits, 1961–1962	
1 Trade Expansion	Impacted Areas
2 Interior Approp.	Mail Propaganda
3 Feed Grains	HEW Approp.
4 Impacted Areas	Manpower
5 HEW Approp.	Housing Act
6 Food & Agric.	Trade Expansion
7 Unemploy. Comp.	Revenue Act
Poorest Fits, 1961–1962	
36 Sugar Act	Sugar Act
35 Mail Prop.	Public Works
34 Cultural Exch.	Maritime Sub.
33 Civil Rights	Literacy
32 Revenue Act	Civil Rights
31 Foreign Assist.	Foreign Assist.
30 Maritime Sub.	Mexican Farm Labor
Best Fits, 1963	
1 Feed Grains	Mass Transit
2 Milk Prod. Control	Feed Grains
3 Vocational Ed.	Nat'l. Serv. Corps
4 Labor-HEW Approp.	Debt. Limit
5 Silver Policy	Fishing Vessels
Poorest Fits, 1963	
25 For. Assist.-Rest.	Defense App.
24 Fishing Vessel	Ind. Off. App.
23 Health Education	For. Assist.-Rest.
22 Ind. Off. App.	Labor-HEW Approp.
21 Defense App.	Cloture Rule

to the bills which are important to the influences in the individual equations. The best fits for the nonsouthern Democrats, whose models exhibited considerable leadership influence, are for many of the bills associated with President Kennedy's New Frontier and foreign policy programs, such as Trade Expansion, Medicare, and

Aid to Education. The importance of the leadership influences and the better fits on bills that were important to the party leadership lends support to the formal leader versions of the organizational model. The southern Democrats and the Republicans, who exhibited strong constituency influences, have their best fits for bills which probably had a high saliency among their electorates. The best example of high constituency related fits is that of the civil rights bills among the southern Democrats. All the civil rights issues are included in the list of bills the individual models are explaining well for the southern Democrats. Similarly, the best fit bills for the Republicans are bills such as Interior Appropriations and extended unemployment compensation for the eastern members, the Housing Act and the banning of Communist propaganda from the mails for the western members, and HEW appropriations, Trade Expansion, and impacted areas school aid for both groups. The observation that southerners and Republicans have their best fits on bills with strong constituency interests supports the representational explanation, which predicts that the constituency model should have its best fits for bills which were important to senators' constituencies. Unfortunately, except for the high saliency of civil rights issues among southern voters, these observations remain speculations lacking adequate data assessing what issues were most important to different constituencies.

There were several interesting bills appearing among the best fit for one group of senators and the poorest fit for another group. There were also interesting cases where a bill was among the best or poorest fit for all but one group of senators, suggesting that the bill evoked different considerations from one particular group of senators. The civil rights bills as a class of legislation best fit the description of bills which were explained well for one group of senators, the southern Democrats, and poorly for others. The efforts to eliminate literacy tests and poll taxes and to liberalize the cloture rule were among the poorest fit bills for western Democrats. The extension of the Civil Rights Commission was poorly fit for both groups of Republicans, while the attempts to abolish literacy tests and change the cloture rule were among the poorest fit bills for western Republicans. This is precisely the illustration used earlier for the sophisticated representational model, and it is consistent with Evans and Novak's reported bargain between Johnson and a western Democrat during consideration of the Civil Rights Act of 1958.

The pattern observed for the civil rights bills was reversed on several issues which may be presumed to have had considerable importance among the western Democrats' states. The west coast maritime subsidy, Medicare, and the appropriations for the Interior Department were among the poorest fit bills for the southern Democrats and among the best fit for their western colleagues (the maritime subsidy was the ninth best fit bill for the western Democrats). The implication is that the western Democrats may have been picking up the support of the southerners on legislation important to western constituencies, particularly the maritime question and the Interior appropriations, in exchange for western votes on issues important to southerners, such as civil rights.

The particularly interesting issue is the question of aid to schools in federally impacted areas. This issue is fairly important to many southern and western constituencies that contain large federal installations. President Kennedy was trying hard to prevent consideration of the impacted areas question except as part of his Aid to Education bill, hoping that the impacted areas money could be used to buy some support for the whole school assistance program. The Republicans, who generally opposed the school assistance proposal on a variety of grounds, wanted separate consideration of the impacted areas question for the opposite reason. The nonsouthern Democrats were generally in favor of the school assistance plan, although support was stronger in the west where the religious question was not so important. (Several eastern Democrats had expressed reservations or opposition to the bill because it did not contain provisions for aid to private and parochial schools.) The western Democrats were trying to prevent separate consideration of the impacted areas question, so as to increase the chances for passage of the school assistance bill, the opposite of the Republican strategy. The poor fit for the southern Democrats on the impacted areas issue could reflect the fact that they had to trade their support or opposition to separate consideration of the impacted areas question, and thus indirectly of the school assistance issue, for western and Republican support on such issues as civil rights.

A very similar pattern was observed for the 1963 voting on attempts to change the cloture rule and on the administration's proposed feed grains program. The equations provide good explanations for the southern Democrats' votes on the cloture issue, but not for the feed grains question. Just the opposite was true for Republicans and western Democrats. The votes of these latter senators were explained quite well for the feed grains plan but poorly for the cloture voting. The results again suggest that Republicans and western Democrats may have been using their votes on civil rights or civil rights related legislation to obtain southern support for positions on legislation that was important to their constituents, and vice versa for southerners.

The bills that were not fit well for the various groups of senators are, for the most part, the bills shown in Tables 6.2 and 6.4 as having poor fits for all senators. Thus, Amendments to the Sugar Quota Act, National Wilderness, Public Works, and Foreign Aid bills were consistently poorly fit for several groups of senators. There were some interesting cases where bills were poorly fit for only one or two groups of senators, such as the civil rights bills among the western Democrats and Republicans. There are also several interesting exceptions where a bill that was poorly fit for several of the groups did not appear on the similar list for another one of the groups. A bill's absence from the list of poorly fit bills for one group suggests that whatever factors contributed to the low fits for the votes of most senators on the particular bill were weaker for this group. For example, the subsidy for the west

coast maritime industry voted in 1962 was poorly fit for eastern
and southern Democrats and all Republicans. This bill did not
appear in the poorly fit list for western Democrats. For the latter
group, it is quite likely that constituency interests were stronger
and better articulated, so that constituencies played a much
larger role and reduced the likelihood of western senators' votes
being influenced by other considerations. The same pattern,
with the deletion of the eastern Republicans from the poorly fit
group, can be observed for the omnibus public works scale constructed from a series of 1961 votes. A reverse pattern is evident
on the trade expansion act of 1962, which was high on the list of
best fit bills for the eastern members of both parties. This again
is not surprising, since the constituencies in these areas would be
the ones most affected by the legislation.

The analysis of the voting behavior of the groups of senators
on the different bills is only suggestive of the appropriateness of
the alternative models of legislative behavior. Some of the bills
that had good fits were certainly indicative of the representational
explanation, such as civil rights among the southern senators. In
other cases, the results were suggestive of the organizational or
party explanations. Many of the bills which were fit best for the
eastern Democrats and some of the ones explained well for the
western Democrats were legislative items being pushed by President Kennedy and presumably getting considerable attention from
the leadership, such as labor legislation and school assistance.
Considering both that the administration bills were being fit well
for the northern Democrats and that the party leaders had a substantial amount of influence among these Democrats, the results
are supportive either of the organizational model emphasizing
the importance of the formal leaders or of the party version of the
coalition model. Support for the organizational model is tempered
somewhat by the fact that many of the bills Kennedy was pushing
and which were fit well for the eastern Democrats, for example,
minimum wage increases, labor legislation, and area redevelop-

ment, undoubtedly had considerable support among their constituents.

There are also patterns of deviation from the individual equations which might have resulted from vote trading by members of
the different regional and party groups. That bills likely to be
important to one group's constituencies were explained well for
senators in that group and poorly for senators from constituencies
where the bill might not be important could be the result of
explicit vote trades among the members of the groups. Senators
who had traded their votes on a bill would exhibit large deviations
from the votes predicted by the systematic component of their
behavior. The more prevalent trading was among the members of
a group on a particular bill, the poorer the fits would be for that
group on the bill. The patterns of vote trading suggested by these
observations, if indicative, support the coalition model of legislative behavior. The coalition behavior did not seem to be dominated
by the behavioral or party version of the coalition model, which
predicted that coalitions would be formed around the party leaders
and that individual senators would vote with the party leaders on
many bills as their contribution to the coalition. Some of the
observed trading, if that was what produced the results, occurred
between members of different parties, such as southern Democrats
and western Republicans. The cross-party vote trading is more
suggestive of pure coalition than of party coalition explanations.

[7] Constituencies, Leaders, and Public Policy

Each of three alternative approaches to legislators' roll call voting behavior, organizational, representational, and trusteeship, proposes different legislative processes and relationships with the external political world, although their predictions about which factors are influential overlap. However, there are subtle differences in the predictions of each explanation about which bills will be explained better, which influences will be stronger, and what the pattern of the important influences will be if one explanation is more powerful than another.

AN EXPLANATION OF SENATE VOTING DECISIONS

Summary of the Results

Senators' constituencies were the most influential variables. Table 4.8 showed that 30 percent of all the senators were best represented by a constituency only model, and only 20 percent did not exhibit any significant constituency influence once the effects of state colleagues were taken into account. (About 10 percent of the senators were not directly influenced by their constituents but were influenced by their state colleague, who, in turn, was responding to constituency influence. See Table 4.7.)

128

Additionally, over half of all senators had constituency coefficients larger than 0.50, and for all groups except the eastern Democrats the magnitudes of the constituency coefficients were considerably larger than any of the organizational coefficients and larger than the *sum* of all the organizational coefficients (see Tables 4.2–4.5). Although Appendix A indicates that the statistical procedures overstate constituency influence relative to organizational influences, the magnitudes of the coefficients in Chapter 4 and in the FAP example in the appendix still indicate that senators' votes have a high probability of following their constituents' positions. There is a strong regional and party pattern to the constituency influences, with Republicans and southern Democrats much more likely than northern Democrats to vote in accord with the positions of the voters back home.

The formal party leaders, represented by the floor leader and whip in each party, were the most important of the organizational variables. Exceptions to this pattern are the western Republicans, for whom the committee variables, particularly the committee conservative influence, were more important. The formal leadership variables were most important among the eastern and western Democrats, although their influence was shared with the committee liberal among eastern Democrats. Half the eastern Democrats and a third of the western ones have significant coefficients for one or both of their party leaders. Over half of the significant coefficients are larger than 0.50, which indicates a sizable influence. Among the northern Democrats, the influence seemed to be evenly divided between Mansfield, the floor leader, and Humphrey, the party whip. There is a noticeable geographic pattern to their influence. Mansfield, from Montana, was more important among the western members of the party, and Humphrey, from Minnesota and the eastern wing of the party, was more influential among the eastern members. In addition, Mansfield has a significant coefficient in Humphrey's equation, indicating that the northern Democrats had a relatively cohesive and influential leadership structure. The Republican leadership, on the other

hand, was both more divided and less influential. Only a fourth
of the Republicans have significant coefficients for their party
leaders, and only one coefficient is greater than 0.50. In addition,
Dirksen, the Republican floor leader, apparently had no influence
on the votes cast by Kuchel, the whip, and Kuchel, in turn, had
virtually no influence among his party colleagues. The Republicans, then, in contrast to the northern Democrats, did not seem to
have very effective floor leadership.

The other important institutional variables were the members
of the reporting committee. Their influence was about evenly
split among the formal committee leaders, the chairman and
ranking Republican, and the informal leaders. These are denoted
as the committee liberal and committee conservative variables.
The coefficients on the informal committee leader variables are
larger, with two-thirds of them being greater than 0.50 (only one
of the formal committee leader coefficients is this large). There
is a noticeable regional pattern among the committee influences,
just as there is among the party leader variables. The formal committee leaders' influence was more likely to be significant among
the western and to some extent among the southern Democrats
and eastern Republicans, while the informal committee leaders
were more likely to effect the votes of the eastern Democrats
and the western Republicans. The members of the latter two
groups had less seniority and therefore were less likely to be
committee chairmen or ranking Republicans. For example, all
the committee chairmen with the exception of Magnuson of
Washington came from the south or southwest. The seniority
differences and the resulting distribution of committee leadership
posts reinforced the obvious constituency and ideological differences between the intraparty groups. The eastern Democrats and
western Republicans were then forced to rely on people other
than the formal committee leaders for information about committee bills and as focal points for subparty coalitions.

The president, who is the last organizational variable, was not
influential on a consistent basis. Kennedy's influence was strongest

among the northern members of his own party. Only seven of them have statistically significant coefficients for the presidential position variable, and none of their coefficients are larger than 0.50. The implication is either that the president did not exert much direct influence on senators' voting decisions, or that the *CQ* reports did a poor job of summarizing the president's position on various bills. The first implication, if true, implies that virtually all organizational influences emanate from within the Senate and that it is the leaders of the president's party who are responsible for pushing the president's legislative program. Of course, the leaders are helped by having the power of the president behind them in close votes. However, neither Democratic floor leader has a significant coefficient for President Kennedy, which suggests that the presidential variable might be in error.

The coefficients which appeared to change between the 1961–62 sessions and the 1963 session, or which were erroneously estimated in the first place as determined by their inability to predict the 1963 votes accurately, were examined for evidence of systematic explanations for the changes. These changes provide further evidence supporting the representational explanation of legislative behavior. The most frequent change is in constituency influence before and after elections. The constituency coefficients drop for several senators following their reelection and increase for many who were one term closer to a campaign. At the same time, there was a slight tendency for the weight accorded organizational influences to increase after an election and to decrease in the session prior to a reelection contest.

A second observed change is in the president's influence among the members of his own party. His influence declined substantially between 1962 and 1963. Several members of the president's party began taking stands contrary to the president's stated positions in 1963, and several senators who supported the president's position in 1961–62 did so less often in 1963. The Democratic senators exhibiting decreased presidential influence were members of the more liberal wing of the Democratic party, such as Prox-

mire, Clark, and Douglas. The most notable exception to the
pattern of decreased presidential influence was not a Democrat,
but Everett Dirksen, the Republican floor leader. Dirksen gave
considerable weight to the president's stated position in 1963,
which was not the case in 1961–62 when he was running for
reelection. This was of little help to the president on floor votes
since Dirksen was not particularly influential on a consistent
basis among the members of his own party.

Deviations from the estimated models are analyzed to ascertain
if they fit one of the explanations of roll call voting. It was observed that the models generally explained less of the voting
behavior of western Democrats than they did for the other groups
of senators. In terms of the individual pieces of legislation, the
models had poorer fits for bills which might be characterized as
special or limited interest bills, such as subsidies for the west
coast maritime industry, sugar quotas, and certain appropriations.

The models' fits on the various bills for each of the groups of
senators were far more revealing than the overall fits for the
specific bills. The most notable differences were on the civil rights
legislation. Naturally, the southern Democrats, given the feelings
of their white constituents on the civil rights issue and the weight
these senators gave to their voting constituency, had their best fits
for these bills. More importantly, in all three sessions, the civil
rights legislation was among the poorest fit bills for the Republicans and the western Democrats. In a contrary fashion, there
were bills such as the impacted areas school aid and the feed grains
program which were among the best fit for Republican and
western Democrats but among the poorest fit for the southern
Democrats.

The results of the bill analysis, both for types of legislation
and for senatorial groups, implies a certain amount and type of
logrolling. Logrolling was predicted between senators whose constituencies are not particularly concerned about issue A but are
interested in issue B and other senators whose constituencies are
adamantly concerned about issue A and who do not care strongly

about issue B. The best examples of such circumstances were civil rights legislation and bills such as west coast maritime subsidies, public works projects, and feed grains proposals. Western senators' constituencies did not have many blacks, and their white constituents were likely more concerned with economic matters relating to natural resources and agricultural issues. Conversely, the voters in southern constituencies were probably much more concerned about civil rights legislation than public works or feed grains. Vote trading between southern Democrats and western senators in both parties would be facilitated by this suggested pattern of concerns. Journalistic accounts of the 1958 Civil Rights Act, some general descriptions of the western Democrats, and the results given in Chapter 6 are consistent with the explanation that some western senators were willing to vote with the southerners on civil rights questions in exchange for some southern support on the bills important to western constituencies.

Selection of a Model

The results discussed throughout this study are inconsistent with a trusteeship approach as well as with both the pure forms of the organizational and representational explanations. The notion that roll call voting has no systematic components or explanations is fairly easy to reject. The overall fits obtained for each senator, as measured by the R^2 for the 1961–62 data, the statistical significances of the coefficients, and finally the predictive power of the equations as measured by the $(1–U^2)$ statistics for the 1963 data should dispel the notion that voting has no systematic antecedents. However, the results do indicate that senators are individuals. There are certain similarities as to what influences are important in senators' voting decisions, particularly within specific party and geographic groups, but there are large differences among the members of the groups. There are variations in the importance of each influence within each group, although these differences are smaller than the variations between groups. The individual models implying that the importance of each influence differs with each senator do substantially better at explaining voting behavior than an alternative explanation, which implies that each senator gives the same weight to constituency and the party leaders but permits the weights to vary with each bill. Thus, senators are individuals, but in terms of how much weight they give to their constituencies, to their party leaders, and to informal leaders and not so much in terms of which influences are important on specific bills.

The large and significant constituency coefficients refute the notion that individual senators do not vote in ways which reflect the preferences of their constituents. (A further illustration of such constituency voting is presented in Appendix A.) Thus, the pure internal or organizational explanations that exclude constituencies would seem to be inadequate. Similarly inadequate is the pure constituency or representational approach. Organizational influences were important, particularly among the northern Democrats, whose members occupied formal leadership positions as the majority party. In addition, a third of the senators do not have significant constituency coefficients, suggesting that a sizable proportion of the Senate is not directly influenced by constituents on a consistent basis. Furthermore, 20 percent of the senators give no evidence of any constituency influence, direct or otherwise. Thus, constituencies are not the sole determinants of senators' votes.

Rejection of both the pure organizational and representational explanations leaves the task of considering a more sophisticated explanation incorporating both the constituency and organizational influences. The one explanation that explicitly includes both influences is the behavioral version of the coalition representational model. This version starts from the straight coalition representational model, which is based on the hypothesis that the probability of legislators voting with their constituents increases as the issue becomes more important to constituent groups, or at least to groups whose support the legislators feel they need for reelection. The legislators trade their votes on the issues where

here are no strong and identifiable groups or interest, or where
he issue is of secondary importance to all members of the con-
tituency to insure the adoption of public policies and programs
vhich are important to their own constituents, thus increasing
heir chances of reelection.

The behavioral version of the coalition explanation accepts
he notion that legislators are trying to trade support and build
coalitions to further their constituents' interest. However, its
proponents argue that given the large demands on legislators'
ime, the resources required to accomplish the bargaining and
ogrolling through individual actions, and the difficulty involved
n keeping agreements reached on legislation considered weeks or
nonths apart, it is in the interest of each legislator to belong to at
east a weakly formed coalition. Then, instead of continually
renegotiating the trades and reestablishing the coalitions, it is
easier to organize the coalitions into parties and to select formal
leaders.

The formal coalition or party leaders function as clearinghouses, or brokers, for the interests of the members. Party leaders
collect votes and promises of support on future legislation from
each member in return for assurance that issues important to
him will receive leadership support. Individual senators then only
have to bargain for support on the bills that are highly important
to them and agree to vote with the leader and the party on most
other legislation. Even though party members can, and undoubtedly do, defect on specific bills where party positions do
not have adequate constituency support, there are strong incentives for legislators to join the party coalitions. Over a period of
time, with stable membership and issues, these coalitions or
parties develop into well structured organizations with formal
leadership structures and set ways of doing business.[1] Once
organized, the parties develop all the functions and characteristics
described by the organizationalists—clearly recognized leaders,
defined roles, and specialization of activity. Also, the coalitions,
or parties, solve the information problem since each coalition

member can develop a well defined set of cue sources within the organization. The important point is that the functions, roles, and responsibilities of the party members and the cue source voting emphasized by organizational models facilitate coalition representational voting behavior and the associated bargaining and trading of support. The coalitions, or parties, supplement but clearly do not entirely replace representational voting.

In addition to the large party coalitions, smaller, less formal coalitions are expected to develop in a body as large and diverse as the senate. The smaller coalitions develop because the formal parties have too wide a distribution of interests and concerns among members to remain cohesive. As the diversity within a party increases, it becomes more likely that constituency concerns will require some members to defect from party positions, or that small groups within the party will feel their positions are not getting enough support. Defectors may then form their own subcoalitions. Subcoalitions may exist on only one or two bills, such as among the Republicans and southern Democrats on civil rights. In other cases they may become almost permanent formal or quasi-formal groups with varying amounts of allegiance to the original party. The southern Democrats are an example of a group which maintained minimal allegiance to the party and voted a straight party line on only a few issues, most notably the votes organizing the senate. The northern Democrats appeared to be constitued of two groups that maintained considerable party allegiance in spite of differences on some issues. One group was the set of more liberal, mostly eastern Democrats who voted with Humphrey and committee members other than the chairmen. The other, mostly western Democrats, generally voted with Mansfield and the committee chairmen.

The predictions of the behavioral version of the coalition representational model are supported by the general importance of the constituency coefficients, by the pattern of influence among the regional and party groups exhibited by the Democratic party leaders and committee members, and by the types of legislation explained well and poorly by the individual models. Versions of the organizational or the representational explanations may be able to account for the significance of both the constituency and leader coefficients. However, the models' fits among the groups of senators for different bills is more consistent with the coalition model, which predicts a general pattern to the fits based on a particular type of vote trading and logrolling. That the bills fit poorly overall and for different groups of senators are those one might consider of limited interest both to citizens generally and to the constituents in the different regions is more consistent with the coalition representational model than with other explanations. At the same time, most of the well-fit bills are ones which might be considered most important to the different constituencies—civil rights bills among southern senators, the feed grains program among Republicans and western Democrats, and employment and labor legislation for the eastern Democrats. At the same time, each of these bills was poorly fit for a different group of senators. The pattern of these fits for groups of senators, as well as the fact that the models generally fit poorly for such issues as the maritime subsidy for the west coast (except for western Democrats), sugar quotas, public works, and space projects, is consistent with the coalition form of the representational model. Constituent concern over these latter special interest bills likely varied on a state by state basis rather than on a regional one, which accounts for the result that votes on these bills were explained poorly for all senators. The fits for the various bills, in addition to indicating the importance of both constituencies and leaders, lends considerable support to the behavioral representational model based on coalition behavior tied to constituency interests.

PUBLIC POLICY, PARTIES, AND REPRESENTATION

It is now appropriate to consider the implications of the coalition representational model of legislative behavior. These implications relate both to descriptive uses of the model and to prescriptive considerations of the role of the legislature in the determination of public policy. Descriptive works on Congress attempt to explain why certain bills pass and what strategies might be employed to pass particular pieces of legislation. The prescriptive implications deal with such questions as congressional reform, whether a national two-party system is possible or desirable, and how legislative districts should be drawn.

Descriptive Implications of the Coalition Representational Model

Explanations for the content of bills and reasons for their passage based on the model place considerable emphasis on the senators' constituents' attitudes, or the perceived impact of the legislation on their constituents, and the constituents' assessment of a bill's importance. As shown in Appendix A, senators' voting on the Family Assistance Plan part of the 1970 Social Security, Trade, and Welfare bill appears to be strongly related to constituency attitudes toward substituting a guaranteed income plan for the current welfare system. In this case, the failure to obtain a family assistance plan in 1970 was attributed to these constituency attitudes. A second explanation suggested by the sophisticated representational model for a bill's content and history once it reaches Congress is that it might have been amended or passed as part of an effort to obtain support for other bills. This bill then is being used to obtain votes for other bills. In such cases, it is difficult to consider the merits of a bill apart from an entire legislative package. For example, a strict interpretation of some public cost benefit analysis may not appear to justify some legislation, such as particular agricultural and public works programs or various economic subsidies. Their passage is usually attributed to the power of special interest groups. However, if these bills are necessary and useful for obtaining sufficient support to pass "general interest" legislation, such as a public housing bill, or minimum wage legislation, etc., whose benefits are also not distributed uniformly, then the appropriate "cost-benefit" calculation must include the costs and benefits of both pieces of legislation. At the same time, passage of the limited interest bill must be attributed, at least in part, to the need to get some additional votes for the other general interest legislation through a series of trades. In some cases such logrolling is appropriate as it is the only way in which the distributional aspects of various public activities can be considered.

The coalition representational model has important implications in the consideration of strategies aimed at passing or defeating particular pieces of legislation. The important variables are the preferences of the senators' constituency and the importance of the legislation to their constituents. If individual legislators can be convinced that their constituencies favor or oppose a bill, they are more likely to vote either for or against it. If it can be established that their constituencies feel a bill is more important than other bills, then the probability of constituency voting is further increased. Increasing a bill's importance also increases the possibility of the bill passing, because the legislators will be more likely to trade their votes on other issues to build support for the bill in question.

Another way to build support for a bill is to obtain the votes of legislators who do not have a strong interest in the particular legislative area by assurances of support for bills which do concern them. Although this is an obvious and undoubtedly much practiced strategy, it has received little systematic examination. This process has remained one of the "arts" of politics. The coalition representational model suggests that one way to encourage bargaining is to have available additional legislation which appeals to the important interests of other legislators and which they will support and be willing to trade some of their votes to get passed. For example, certain types of issues which benefit some constituencies more than others can be used to "buy" votes in support of the legislation in question. Certainly many organizational explanations indicate that some senators, particularly the leaders, buy votes, but they are often referring to nonlegislative considerations, such as personal benefits or committee assignments,[2] and seldom to legislation which is connected with constituency interests.

The empirical results and the model of legislative behavior which they support should be most welcome to people who argue that legislators should represent their individual constituents and that one of the functions of the legislature is to recognize and deal with the various legitimate conflicts inherent in public policy issues. The results are less comforting to those who want legislators to be members of uniform national parties and who see Congress as an institution where alternative legislative programs are developed and considered.

NORMATIVE IMPLICATIONS OF THE COALITION REPRESENTATIONAL MODEL

The findings imply quite different strategies of governmental reform depending upon one's normative view. People who want a unified party system of government where alternative party platforms are debated, voted on, and the winning one executed will want to strengthen the national party conventions, general elections, and the office of the president. In this plan, Congress becomes a place to debate presidential policy and less of a policy-making body. In contrast, those who feel that policies require negotiations among the various interested individuals and groups, that coalitions and their associated trades and side payments are a necessary part of government, and that minority interests are best accounted for by having someone associated with and accountable to those interests actively involved in the policy setting process will favor increasing Congress's role. Policies and priorities then are established by Congress and it is Congress's responsibility to make sure they are executed properly.

Some form of logrolling in the public sector is a desirable and, in fact, necessary process as well as an observable phenomenon.[3] The collective nature of the decisions being made by the legislature is at the core of this necessity. Most of the issues considered by legislatures affect large groups of people. Individuals attach quite different values to the outcomes of these decisions, however. If people could independently pursue their own policies and engage in the kind of activities they want without regard to what other people are doing, the differences in valuation would not be a problem and questions of logrolling and coalitions, as well as discussions of public agencies, would be irrelevant. A process of private decision-making is not possible, or at least not desirable, on such issues as foreign aid, the environment, and civil rights, so the decisions must be made collectively.

Every decision about a collective activity has significant distributional impacts. As an illustration, although programs like public housing, flood control and irrigation, mass transit, and national defense may benefit everyone, they are more highly valued by specific groups within the population, while the distribution of their costs is determined by the federal tax structure. It is usually impossible to relate the incidence of these taxes to the benefits of specific programs. Thus, people in Montana are paying some of the costs for urban housing, education, and job-training programs, just as city dwellers contribute to the cost of agricultural price supports and public power projects. Even national defense, which does not usually evoke images of regional or geographic benefits, is similar in that people in different parts of the country, for a variety of reasons, have different ideas about how much and what types of defense expenditures are required. Consequently, even proposals to change the defense budget have distributional implications. These distributional considerations apply to symbolic issues as well as questions of an economic nature. All public policy questions involve decisions of a collective nature which favor some groups and are possibly detrimental to others. Regardless of the type of issue, these interests need to be recognized and taken into account in the making of public policy decisions.

The vote trading and coalition formation found in this study of the senate combine various programs with their different benefit distributions into packages, so that people who are being asked to pay for a program from which they receive few benefits are promised other public services which they do value in return. In terms of this study, people in Idaho received public power and silver subsidies at the same time they were paying part of the cost of urban mass transit; farmers in North Dakota received farm price supports and acreage controls while paying for economic development in West Virginia; and so on. It would be economically more efficient if a way could be found to tax in proportion to the benefits received. For example, the tax rate for commuters and other urban dwellers might increase to pay for mass transit. Regardless of its desirability for some people such a system is neither feasible nor realistic due to the nature of public activities, governmental institutions, and tax instruments. It is necessary to rely on other desired public activities to provide the side payments and compensations.

Vote trades and coalitions do not always operate to increase the amount of public activity. Some people will be more concerned about defeating particular legislation or stopping some programs. They will be willing to support or oppose the bills which concern other people in order to build opposition to the bills they want defeated. Trading to defeat legislation is best illustrated by the way southern Democrats were willing to support legislation important to other senators to build opposition to civil rights bills, and by Republican efforts to defeat school assistance by getting other senators to agree to separate consideration of aid for impacted areas.

This discussion is certainly not intended to imply that all the logrolls and vote trades which the senate made in 1961, 1962, and 1963, or in any other year, are appropriate, in the national interest, or even in the interest of most constituencies. It is merely saying that some logrolling is necessary, and that this study indicates the senate does seem to engage in vote trading.[4] One would have to know individual constituents' preferences and how strongly they feel about issues, as well as precisely what trades take place, before making a value judgment.[5] This argument does suggest, however, that care must be taken in determining what is considered special interest legislation, or "pork." Public power or a reclamation project may not be any more "pork" to a western state concerned about its economic development than is public housing to an urban area or mass transit to suburban commuters.

The legislature is the branch of government which should determine the trades, or bundles of specific programs, containing the side payments required to take account of distributional questions. Kendall and Carey make the point that the logrolls and coalitions also are the only way in which a democratic society can take into account individuals' and minorities' intensities on different issues and weigh as well as count preferences.[6] Vote trades are expressions of such intensities. Haefele and Rothenberg argue that the legislature is the best place, and the individual legislators the most appropriate officials, for making the trades and determining the side payments required by minority interests and the differential impacts of policy decisions.[7] Legislators are not associated with the administration of particular services, and ideally their futures are dependent upon their representational ability and on their skill in negotiating the coalitions required to implement desired policies, not on their ability to administer and promote specific programs.[8] For this observed system to function well, Congress must be able to accurately evaluate the consequences of different policy proposals and ascertain the implications and impacts of the programs and expenditures it considers. At the same time, in order to make the constituency voting exhibited by senators effective, voters must elect legislators on the basis of their performance in representing constituency concerns in the policy-making process and on their voting behavior in the course of trading support and forming coalitions on different bills. Recognition of their responsibilities both by Congress and by the voters can only lead to better performance of the functions Congress is seen executing and to improved public policies.

Appendixes, Notes, Index

Appendix A. The Development of the Constituency Variables

The assumption was made during the construction of the constituency variables that constituency opinion can be inferred from the systematic relationship between senators' votes on a given bill and the demographic characteristics of their states. There are several ways to examine the validity of this assumption and its implications for estimating senators' voting behavior. One approach is empirical. If it is possible to directly measure constituency support for a piece of legislation without resort to the senators' actual votes, this support variable can be examined for how well it explains senate voting behavior and how well it correlates with a constituency variable as constructed in Chapter 3. If this direct estimate of constituency support both explains senate voting behavior well and correlates highly with the indirectly estimated senate constituency variable, it should increase confidence in the indirect procedure used in Chapter 3. Alternatively, the estimation problem can be examined analytically. This approach develops a formal statistical model to represent the procedure used in constructing the constituency variable and in estimating senators' models. The formal model then shows how the procedures affect the estimates of the coefficients in the

147

senatorial voting equations. This appendix follows both approaches.

EXAMPLE: SENATE VOTING ON THE FAMILY ASSISTANCE PLAN[1]

President Nixon's proposed Family Assistance Plan (FAP) will be used to compare the constituency variables. The initial effort to enact FAP terminated on December 28, 1970, when the senate voted 49–21 to kill the part of HR 17550 dealing with the president's FAP proposal as amended by Senator Ribicoff and other senate liberals.

Senate floor consideration of FAP was entangled in parliamentary maneuvering and filibustering over an omnibus bill relating to Social Security, Medicare and Medicaid, and trade quota provisions, as well as welfare reform. On December 18, Senator Ribicoff offered an amendment to this bill. The amendment, which was also sponsored by Senator Wallace Bennett (R., Utah), was a modified version of the administration FAP plan. The following day the senate defeated by a 65–15 roll call vote a motion by Senator Long to table the Ribicoff amendment. Then on December 28, Long moved that the whole bill be returned to committee with instructions to report back only those sections dealing with Social Security, Medicare and Medicaid, and specific reforms in the existing welfare legislation. Two of these changes would have reestablished man-in-the-house and residency requirements, which the Supreme Court had previously struck down. These regulations are, of course, absent from all FAP proposals as well. Senator Harris then moved that the committee also be instructed to remove all of the sections of the bill dealing with welfare. This motion was defeated on a 42–27 roll call vote. The Long recommittal motion then passed by the 49–21 vote.

Estimating Senate and Constituency Support for FAP

Each senator's support for the concept of a Family Assistance Plan is measured by a Guttman scale constructed from the three roll call votes. Inclusion of the Harris motion means the variable might be better labeled a measure of support for welfare reform. However, since the enactment of FAP certainly would lighten eligibility requirements and prevent the residency and man-in-the-house criteria, one can argue that the above votes do relate to the degree of support for family assistance. Senators in the top group voted to consider FAP, supported the Harris amendment, and voted against the Long tabling motion. The next group of 39 senators voted for the tabling motion but voted with Harris, and for senate consideration of the plan. Senators in the lowest group voted against even considering the FAP proposal. This last group, of course, also voted against the Harris motion and supported the Long move to delete even the limited experiment. Each of the four groups of senators are simply assigned an integer score reflecting their position. These scores range from zero, indicating no support and a vote against considering the proposal, to three, reflecting maximum support and a vote against the Long recommittal motion. Table A.1 shows the distribution of senators by scale score. Eighty-three senators cast a sufficient number of votes to be scalable and 247 votes were included in the analysis. This number includes pairs and announced votes. This is a good scale by most conventional standards, since only six votes did not fit the scale pattern.[2]

An estimate of the amount of support for the Family Assistance Plan in each state can be estimated with 1970 Census Bureau data and the responses to a survey taken by the Survey Research Center of the University of Michigan in the fourth quarter of 1969. One of the questions in this survey was: "Some say that welfare should be replaced by a system in which the government

TABLE A.1. DISTRIBUTION OF SCALE SCORES ON THE FAP
GUTTMAN SCALE

Score	0	1	2	3
Number of senators	13	39	14	17

raises the income of the poor so that every family in the country would have an income at least equal to some minimum poverty standard. What do you think of this proposal?" Responses were coded in the following fashion,

1. Good idea.
2. Good idea, with qualifications (if they make it fair; if they make person work, etc.).
3. Pro-con.
4. Bad idea (other reason, or NA why); bad because . . .
5. Too expensive a plan.
6. Impossible to do; can't fairly decide who needs it and some people would take advantage of it.
7. DK (don't know, undecided).
8. NA (no answer).

These responses were recoded into the trichotomous categories of Favorable (items 1, 2), Unfavorable (items 4, 5, 6), and No Opinion (items 3, 7, 8). Of the total sample, 46 percent favored the plan, 13 percent had no expressed opinion, and 41 percent opposed it. Thus, a very high proportion of the respondents (87 percent) expressed an opinion on the basic idea underlying FAP. The remainder of this analysis will concentrate solely on those individuals who expressed an opinion.

This survey, with only 1469 respondents, is not designed as a representative random sample of the opinion within each state. The respondents can be classified by race, region, and metro-politan or rural place of residence, and by income for whites only. The black sample is not large enough to permit a stratification by income. The survey is presumably a representative sample of people within these categories. Thus, the support for FAP among the people sampled within each racial, regional, residential, and income category should be indicative of the proportion of the total population of each group favoring the plan. The classifications and their respective proportions favoring FAP are shown in Tables A.2 and A.3.

TABLE A.2. PROPORTION OF WHITES FAVORING FAMILY ASSISTANCE PLAN

Whites	Urban income						Rural income					
	< 3	3–5	5–7.5	7.5–15	15–25	> 25	< 3	3–5	5–7.5	7.5–15	15–25	> 25
West												
Favorable %	0.90	0.57	0.64	0.43	0.67	0.00	0.72	0.56	0.42	0.39	0.50	0.00
Cell size	10	7	11	30	3	1	18	16	31	67	18	3
North Central												
Favorable %	1.00	0.60	0.25	0.53	0.82	0.40	0.69	0.55	0.50	0.40	0.43	0.10
Cell size	3	5	8	45	11	5	42	31	38	103	28	10
North East												
Favorable %	0.83	0.63	0.47	0.62	0.50	0.62	0.64	0.58	0.52	0.45	0.50	0.67
Cell size	12	8	19	60	16	13	11	12	23	74	8	3
South												
Favorable %	0.40	0.83	0.36	0.36	0.50	0.29	0.58	0.50	0.59	0.39	0.39	0.14
Cell size	5	6	11	28	12	7	43	38	66	94	23	7

TABLE A.3. PROPORTION OF BLACKS FAVORING FAMILY
ASSISTANCE PLAN

Blacks	West		N.C.		N.E.		South	
	Urb.	Rur.	Urb.	Rur.	Urb.	Rur.	Urb.	Rur.
Favorable %	0.69	0.67	0.90	0.68	0.90	1.00	0.85	0.59
Cell size	16	3	10	25	19	2	13	41

   With one additional assumption, the data in Tables A.2 and A.3
can be used to construct a measure of constituency support for
FAP in each state. The Census Bureau has prepared 1970 census
data for each state giving the distribution of whites and nonwhites
by metropolitan or rural residence and the income distributions
of white and nonwhite families and of metropolitan and rural
families but not of metropolitan and rural white families. This
last stratification is required to completely match the categories
in Tables A.2 and A.3. In order to overcome this deficiency, white
income distributions for metropolitan and nonmetropolitan areas
are estimated from the available data. Within each income category, the distribution of whites between metropolitan and rural
areas is assumed to be the same as that for all the people in that
income category. For example, if 60 percent of all the state's
families in an income category live in metropolitan areas, then it
was assumed that 60 percent of the white families in that income
class lived in metropolitan areas. This assumption is made for all
the income categories shown in Table A.2. From these calculations,
the percentage distribution of whites by income class in both the
metropolitan and nonmetropolitan areas of each state is estimated.
   The above approximation of the white income distribution by
place of residence makes the construction of the constituency
variable straightforward. The state's population is now grouped
into the same categories used to construct Table A.2. The proportions in Table A.2 are a measure of the proportion of the

people within each category in each state who favor FAP; they permit estimation of the percent of the state's total population that favors substituting FAP for the existing welfare program.[3] Although there are problems inherent in this procedure, the estimates it gives appear to be the best that can be obtained from available data.

The paper dealing explicitly with the FAP, explored in some detail the relationships between senators' voting and constituency preferences along with the influences of party membership and presidential aspirations. Analysis of the residuals from a straight party, region, and constituency model suggested both that the Democratic presidential aspirants supported a stronger position than predicted by the attitudes of their state constituencies and that some senators gave different weights to the preferences of their black constituents. The final result is a model which explains each senator's votes on the FAP legislation on the basis of party membership, potential candidacy for the 1972 Democratic presidential nomination, and several constituency variables. The first constituency variable is simply the proportion of the states' population which favored substituting FAP for the current welfare plan, and the second measures the percentage of the nonwhite population that favored the plan multiplied by the proportion of the state's population that was nonwhite. The model is specified so that the coefficient on this last variable is different for southern Democrats, northern Republicans, and all other senators (northern Democrats and the five southern and border Republicans). The estimated coefficients are shown in Table A.4.[4]

The strong association between the constituency variable and senators' positions on FAP is evident. This is consistent with the results discussed in Chapter 4, where constituency was a consistently important influence for most senators. More significant for consideration of the constituency variable developed in Chapter 3 is the fact that the constituency variable in Table A.3 is merely a weighted sum of the proportion of each state's population with different demographic characteristics. One such charac-

TABLE A.4. COEFFICIENTS IN THE EQUATION EXPLAINING SENATE VOTING ON FAP

Variable	Coefficient	Standard error
Constant	−8.58	2.37
Republican (R)	−0.91	0.41
Presidential candidate (P)	1.46	0.53
Constituency (C)	21.56	4.79
Nonwhite preference (N)	−9.57	4.23
Southern Democrat * Nonwhite preference (S * N)	−8.15	4.09
Republican * nonwhite Preference (R * N)	7.52	5.05
$V_1{}^a$	0.00	—
$V_2{}^a$	2.53	0.37
$V_3{}^a$	3.52	0.43

[a]The V's are the estimated cutting points implicit in the Guttman scale, with V_1 = 0.00 by construction. The estimated equation gives a predicted value for each senator based upon constituency values, party, etc. The estimated cutting points are then used to group the senators. For example, a senator with an estimated value less than 0.00 would be assigned to group 1, a senator with a value between 0.00 and 2.53 to group 2, and so on.

teristic is the percentage of the white population living in metropolitan areas and earning between 7.5 and 15 thousand dollars. The weights, of course, are the proportion of the members of each demographic group expected to favor the FAP proposal. They are derived from the SRC survey and are independent of senators' votes. The constituency variable developed in Chapter 3 is also based on a weighting of the demographic characteristics of the state, but the weights are derived from the relationship between senator's votes and the demographic variables rather than from a survey.

There are two other results of the FAP study which are relevant to this discussion of the alternative constituency variables. The first is the different weights accorded the preferences of non-whites and the implication that southern Democrats virtually ignored these citizens' opinions.[5] The other relevant result is that the Democratic presidential aspirants supported the plan to a greater extent than would be predicted in the basis of constituency attitudes. These additional results are important in constructing the constituency variable for FAP by the procedure discussed in Chapter 3.

Inferring a FAP Constituency Variable from Senator's Votes

It is a fairly straightforward task to compute a constituency variable for the FAP legislation using the process described in Chapter 3. Most of the variables shown in Table 3.3 are available in the 1970 census. The only ones not available were Farm Bureau and Farm Union membership, which are deleted from the comparison. The equation used to estimate the constituency variable differs from the one used in Chapter 3 in two ways. First, the Democratic presidential aspirant variable shown in Table A.3 is added to the equation. Previous results show that the senators vying for the Democratic presidential nomination in 1972 took a more favorable position on FAP than would be indicated by their state constituency's attitudes. Their positions were undoubtedly designed to appeal more to a particular national constituency than to their state constituency. The presidential aspirant variable accounts for these systematic deviations from constituency positions. This particular effect was not a problem in 1961–1963, of course, when it was expected that President Kennedy would be seeking a second term. Second, instead of basing the constituency characteristic variables only on the white population for the southern states, as was done in Chapter 3, a black variable was included in the constituency equation. This variable was specified as the percentage black in each state and designed so that it would have a negative effect on the voting of southern Democrats and a positive effect on the voting of the remaining senators. Table A.4 supports the hypothesis set forth in Chapter 3 that the positions

of the white constituents was the relevant constituency variable
for explaining the votes of southern Democrats. Including blacks
in the southern states' demographic variables overstates the
support for FAP among the southern white constituents because
blacks favored the plan more than whites. Including the per-
centage-of-blacks variable with a negative effect for the southern
Democrats adjusts for this overstatement of the relevant constituency positions. Otherwise, the same variables and procedures
used to construct the constituency variables in Chapter 3 are
followed for the FAP votes.

The procedure for constructing this constituency variable is
simple, although it may sound complicated. The value of one is
added to each of the senator's scale scores so that the scales
ranged from one to four. This eliminates the zero values so it is
possible to take the log of each senator's score, as is required by
the functional form used in Chapter 3.[6] The new values, the log of
the scale scores plus one, are then regressed against the reciprocals
of the demographic variables describing each constituency. The
results of the regression are shown in Table A.5. The point was
made in Chapter 3, and should be reiterated here, that these coefficients should not be interpreted in any causal sense. The
information in Table A.2 and A.3 indicates that opinion on FAP
varies with each income class as well as by residence, race, and
possibly by region. However, the equation estimated in Table A.5
only includes one income variable, and its coefficient is not
estimated separately for each region and for metropolitan and
rural areas as required by the differences shown in Tables A.2
and A.3. Although these omissions clearly constitute a misspecification of the actual equation relating constituencies' demographic
characteristics and opinions, the effect of the misspecification
will be picked up by the other variables in the equation. For
example, the education and occupation variables in Table A.5
undoubtedly represent the effect of the missing income effects.
As long as the variables in the equation and their coefficients are
not interpreted in a causal sense, the omissions do not present a

TABLE A.5. ESTIMATED CONSTITUENCY EQUATION BASED ON
SENATORS' VOTES[a]

Variable[b]	Coefficient	t-Statistic
Intercept	12.29	1.45
Border	−0.35	−2.18
Midwest	−0.05	−0.29
South	−0.43	−1.92
Southwest	−0.67	−4.36
West	−0.07	−0.43
% Metropolitan	−0.01	−0.47
% High school, but no college[c]	−89.17	−2.64
% Farmer[c]	−264.00	−2.01
% Manager[c]	−276.22	−0.55
% Clerical, Sales[c]	−28.58	−0.40
% Laborer[c]	−97.49	−1.66
% Income over $15,000	−1.60	−0.47
% Over 55	−2.74	−0.36
% Unemployed[c]	−160.76	−0.39
% Black (except southern Democrats)	0.00	0.06
% Black (southern Democrats)[c]	−41.02	−2.58
Democratic presidential aspirant	0.56	4.58
$R^2 = 0.69$		

[a]Dependent variable is the log of the senator's scale score plus one.

[b]The college education and income between $10,000 and $15,000 variables omitted. They were too highly correlated with the included variables to permit their inclusion in the above equations.

[c]These variables are included as the reciprocal of one hundred minus the variable, $1/(100 - Z)$, to indicate that increases in the proportion of the population in this category lead to decreased senatorial support for FAP. For example, z_7 is the percentage of the population with a high school education but no college. The variable in the above equation is $1/(100 - z_7)$, so that support for FAP decreases as z_7 increases.

problem. The important question is simply how well the positions of the senators from each state predicted by this equation correspond to the constituency variable estimated from the SRC survey.

The estimated constituency position for each senator is the senator's predicted scale score from the equation in Table A.5 with the effect of the Democratic presidential aspirant variable deleted. Because of the log transformation, this predicted scale score is the antilog, or exponential, of the predicted value of the dependent variable in this equation minus one. In formal terms, if $\hat{Y}$ is the predicted value of the dependent variable in the equation in Table A.5, then the estimated constituency variable is $(e^{\hat{Y}} - 1.0)$. This replicates the procedure described in Chapter 3, which was used to construct the constituency variables for the 1961–63 legislation.

The important question is how well the two different constituency variables correspond to each other. If one accepts the notion that a constituency variable based on the responses to an individual survey better represent the positions of senators' constituencies, then a high correlation between these two constituency variables should make one somewhat more comfortable about the variables used in the study. This comfort must be qualified, because FAP is only one piece of legislation and there is no way of knowing how representative it is. One comparison is better than none, however.

Estimates of the constituency position for only forty-seven of the states are available from Table A.5 because there were three states where both senators were absent from the voting. It is then a simple matter to correlate the estimated positions for each of the states obtained from Table A.1 with the proportion of the state's population favoring passage of the family assistance legislation estimated from the survey. In the case of the south, the latter variable is based solely on the percent of the white population estimated to favor the plan. This is consistent with the procedure in Chapter 3 which bases the constituency demographic variables only on characteristics of the white population, and with the results of the FAP study which showed that southern Democrats gave virtually no weight to the preferences of nonwhites in their constituencies. For the nonsouthern states the percent favoring FAP was computed on the basis of the entire population. The simple correlation between the two constituency variables for the forty-seven states was 0.85. Thus, there is considerable correspondence between two constituency variables constructed by quite different procedures.

There is an important implication in these results if the FAP legislation is representative of the bills used in the study of the senate in 1961–1963. In the case of FAP, an available survey had asked a question which matched the question Congress was considering—"Should the current welfare system be replaced by a program which guarantees that each family's income will be raised to some minimum standard?" The individual responses to this question could then be used to construct a constituency variable which is directly related to the issue on which the votes were cast. This constituency variable is not only an important predictor of senators' votes on the FAP proposal but is also highly correlated with the variable derived from the association between these senators' votes and the characteristics of their states' populations. If the FAP legislation is at all representative, the results imply that the constituency variables estimated for the 1961–63 bills may be highly correlated with variables which could have been constructed from survey data if the appropriate questions had been asked in the early sixties.

THE FORMAL STATISTICAL MODEL

An alternative way of examining the process used to construct the constituency variables and to estimate each senator's voting model is to use a formal statistical model of the estimating procedures. This section develops such a model. In its mathematical form, this model is used to examine the difficulties involved in the procedures. The statistical model is also used to build a simple monte carlo simulation of the estimating process. The results of this simulation should provide a clear picture of the importance and influence of these difficulties.

The main ingredients in the formal model are the mathematical representations of the legislative voting process, the important influences in this process, and the relationships between the influences and the voting decisions. The model represents a legislature with N legislators taking positions on M different bills. These positions are systematically related to the positions of different leaders, the preferences of the various constituencies, and the weight each legislator gives to these influences. For the sake of simplicity, leaders are assumed to be outside the group of N legislators. Constituency opinion on each bill is assumed to be related to the demographic characteristics of the constituency in a linear fashion, rather than the log-reciprocal form used in Chapter 3 and in the FAP example. The notation used to represent these legislators and their voting behavior is shown in Figure A.1.

For senator j, the relationship between his position on each bill and the positions of the relevant leaders and his constituency's position is written as

$$(A.1) \quad V_j = YA_j + X_j C_j + U_j$$

where V_j is a column vector of his votes on each bill; Y is a series of column vectors representing the positions of each leader; A_j is a column vector of the weights which senator j gives each leader; X_j is the column vector of constituency positions on each bill—the percentage favoring FAP, for example; C_j is the influence constituency has on senator j; and U_j represents the random deviations in j's voting behavior. There will be N such equations, one for each legislator. The N equations can be represented by a single expression,

$$(A.2) \quad V = YA + XC + U.$$

V is now a matrix of votes where each colum is a different legislator, or conversely, the rows of V are the positions of each legislator on a given bill; each column of A is the leadership weights of a different legislator; C is a diagonal matrix with each senator's constituency coefficient on the diagonal and zeroes elsewhere;

predicted position on each bill. This predicted value is the estimate of the senator's constituency position on each bill.

The hypothesized voting model for senator j is then estimated by regressing his positions on each bill against the positions of the leaders included in his model and the estimated constituency variable, $\hat{X}_j$. The equation being estimated is

$$(A.7) \quad V_j = YA_j + \hat{X}_j C_j + U_j + e_j C_j,$$

where $e_j = X_j - \hat{X}_j$. The difference between this and Eq. A.1 is that the estimated constituency variable, $\hat{X}_j$, has been substituted for the true variable, X_j. This substitution necessitates the inclusion of the additional error term $C_j e_j$, since the estimated and true constituency variables will not coincide.

The important question is whether the addition of this new error term, $U_j + e_j C_j$, to the model will affect the estimates of the coefficients A_j and C_j, and if it does, to what extent. The mathematical note to this appendix shows that the estimated coefficients in Eq. A.7 are not unbiased and that the bias is related to the amount of variance in the error terms in the legislator's voting equations, the magnitude of the individual's constituency coefficient, and the correlation between the leadership effects on each bill, YA, and the constituency demographic variables, Z. Unfortunately, the equations expressing these relationships are too complex to show easily the magnitudes of these difficulties and their possible severity.

Simulating the Estimation Procedure[7]

In addition to being intractable, the expressions in the mathematical note to this appendix are not entirely representative of the estimation process used here. The development of the constituency variable in Chapter 3 assumed both a nonlinear relationship between constituency opinion and the demographic constituency variables and used a nonlinear form for the estimated constituency opinion variable. These transformations, when combined with the difficulty of interpreting the expressions in the mathematical note, make it difficult to see precisely how these problems will affect the results discussed earlier.

To provide a better grasp of how the results reported in Chapters 4–6 are effected by this estimation procedure, a small monte carlo simulation of the statistical procedure is developed. Since the true coefficient values are known at the beginning of the simulation, they can be compared with the estimated coefficients. Also, the simulation provides a chance to vary the magnitude of the problems uncovered by the formal analysis, enabling one to measure the sensitivity of the estimates.

The procedure for estimating both the constituency variables and each senator's voting model is simulated in a straightforward fashion by constructing a small legislature represented by specific values for each of the matrices in Eq. A.2 and Fig. A.1. This is done by specifying twenty senators ($N = 20$), twenty bills ($M = 20$), and two leaders ($L = 2$). The twenty senators are divided so that the first ten are influenced by the first leader and the rest by the second leader. Within each group of ten, half the members have high leadership and low constituency coefficients while the opposite holds for the other half. These leader and constituency coefficients specify both the A and C matrices in Eq. A.2 and are shown in Table A.6. Leader positions are selected so that the second leader takes a stronger stand on most bills than the first. The constituency opinion model is based on two demographic variables describing each constituency. Specifying a constituency position for each bill simply means selecting the coefficients used to weight these demographic characteristics in determining each constituency's position on each bill, the B_i's in Eq. A.3. The positions of each leader, the constituency model coefficients, and the values of the demographic variables are also shown in Tables A.6 and A.7.

Running the simulation is quite simple. The log-reciprocal relationship between constituency characteristics and constituency position is used here to construct the actual constituency position

TABLE A.6. LEGISLATOR INPUT TO SIMULATIONS

Legislator	Leader coefficients		Constituency coefficient	Demographic variables	
	$A_{1,j}$	$A_{2,j}$	C_j	$Z_{1,j}$	$Z_{2,j}$
1	0.79	0.00	0.08	0.62	0.78
2	0.89	0.00	0.00	0.62	0.76
3	0.98	0.00	0.13	0.32	0.58
4	0.65	0.00	0.00	0.96	0.54
5	0.62	0.00	0.00	0.82	0.54
6	0.09	0.00	0.96	0.32	0.92
7	0.00	0.00	0.93	0.58	0.38
8	0.11	0.00	0.76	0.36	0.70
9	0.00	0.00	0.89	0.60	0.56
10	0.14	0.00	0.83	0.60	0.42
11	0.00	0.93	0.07	0.46	0.52
12	0.00	0.57	0.00	0.72	0.28
13	0.00	0.99	0.00	0.60	0.80
14	0.00	0.62	0.03	0.30	0.80
15	0.00	0.72	0.14	0.78	0.46
16	0.00	0.00	0.61	0.56	0.70
17	0.00	0.09	0.94	0.66	0.64
18	0.00	0.05	0.63	0.58	0.68
19	0.00	0.00	0.54	0.62	0.56
20	0.00	0.00	0.74	0.58	0.44

on each bill. The systematic part of the constituency positions is estimated from the reciprocals of the demographic variables for each constituency, $1/Z_1$ and $1/Z_2$, and the bill coefficients, B_0, B_1, and B_2, shown in Table A.6. An error term drawn from a normal population with variance σ_w^2 is then added to each term to correspond to Eq. A.4. This term represents the fact that constituency position will not be an exact function of the constituency demographic characteristics. The constituency position on each bill, then, is the exponential of the sum of the error term and systematic component, conforming to the nonlinear, log-recip-

TABLE A.7. BILL INPUT TO SIMULATIONS

Bill	Positions of leaders		Constituency model coefficients		
	$Y_{i,1}$	$Y_{i,2}$	Constant $B_{i,0}$	Variable $B_{i,1}$	Variable $B_{i,2}$
1	1	4	3.8	0.70	0.74
2	2	4	4.4	0.83	0.73
3	0	3	4.1	0.71	0.72
4	0	2	4.0	0.72	0.80
5	0	3	4.2	0.74	0.80
6	1	3	4.1	0.83	0.76
7	3	2	3.9	0.78	0.82
8	2	4	4.0	0.82	0.77
9	1	1	3.9	0.74	0.72
10	1	3	4.0	0.84	0.76
11	1	2	3.6	0.78	0.77
12	1	4	4.4	0.74	0.72
13	1	4	4.4	0.71	0.84
14	2	4	3.5	0.74	0.78
15	1	2	4.1	0.76	0.84
16	1	3	4.4	0.73	0.76
17	2	4	4.1	0.82	0.84
18	1	4	3.9	0.78	0.77
19	1	4	4.1	0.71	0.81
20	1	4	3.6	0.82	0.78

rocal hypothesis. For example, the position of the first constituency on bill one is $EXP(3.8 - 0.70/0.62 - 0.74/0.78 + W_{11})$.

Once constituency positions are calculated, actual positions of each legislator are determined from the positions taken by the appropriate leader times the weight the legislator gives to that leader plus his constituency coefficient times the constituency position on each bill plus an error term drawn from a normal population with variance σ_u^2. This summation corresponds to Eq. A.1, and the error term represents the legislator's deviation from his systematic voting pattern and corresponds to the

U term in Eq. A.1. For example, the position of the first legislator on the first bill was, $V_{11} = (0.79)(1) + (0.08)\,EXP(3.8 - 1.13 - 0.95 + W_{11}) + U_{11}$. This is done for each legislator on each bill to complete the V matrix.

A constituency position on each bill for each legislator is estimated by regressing the log of the legislator's positions on each bill against the reciprocals of each constituency demographic variable. The value of the exponential, or antilog, of the fitted values from these regressions becomes the constituency variables. The coefficients in the voting model of each legislator are estimated by regressing his positions against the positions taken by the appropriate leader and the estimated constituency variable. This whole process, starting with the determination of the constituency positions, is repeated twenty times, using different error terms both for the constituency equation, $X = BZ + W$, and for each senator's voting equation, $V = YA + XC + U$. These twenty replications yield twenty estimates of the coefficients in each senator's voting model. The average of these coefficients can be compared with the true values of the coefficients given in Table A.6 to give a measure of the bias in the estimating procedure. The estimated variance of these coefficients can also be computed with each regression. A t-statistic is then computed and compared with the critical value at the 5 percent level. A score is kept of the number of times the null hypothesis of no influence is rejected in favor of the conclusion that the variable has either a positive or a negative influence. Thus, in addition to an idea of the bias in the estimates, the simulation gives an idea of how conclusions about whether different variables are important are affected by the statistical procedure.

The simulation is run with different values for the variances of both W and U (the error terms in the constituency and voting models) and for two different degrees of correlation between the leadership effects and the constituency demographic variables. The high correlation case was obtained by giving the ten legislators associated with the first leader the constituencies with the lowest values of Z_1 and Z_2, and the second ten the highest values of Z_1 and Z_2. The voting models of each legislator are the same in both simulations. The different simulations should provide an idea of how the estimated coefficients are effected by these problems.

Tables A.8–A.11 show the results of the simulations. The average bias in the estimated coefficients are shown in Table A.8. These biases are shown separately for those legislators with different leader and constituency coefficients. The most apparent result is that the leadership coefficients are consistently underestimated (the entries are estimated values minus true value, so that a negative difference indicates an underestimate), and the constituency coefficients are consistently overestimated. As predicted by the development in the mathematical note, these biases are greater in the simulation with a high correlation between the leadership effects and the constituency demographic variables and for the legislators with large constituency coefficients. The pattern of the biases with changes in the error variances do not completely conform to the predictions. The biases consistently increase with increases in the voting model error variances, σ_u, but only for the legislators with low constituency and high leader coefficients. The reverse effect is apparent for legislators with low leadership and high constituency coefficients—the biases decreased as σ_u increased. Increases in the variances in the constituency opinion model, σ_w, cause just the opposite effects. As the variance of W increases, the bias in the coefficients decreases for legislators with low constituency coefficients and increases for those with high constituency coefficients. The fact that the biases are related to the size of the constituency coefficient means that legislators with a large constituency influence have this influence more overstated than legislators with a small constituency influence, and small leadership influences are more understated than large leader influences. Thus, the worst cases of bias tend to exaggerate only the important constituency variables and diminish the unimportant leadership variables.

TABLE A.8. AVERAGE BIASES

Error term standard deviations		Leader coefficients				Constituency coefficients			
		Moderate correlation[a]		High correlation[a]		Moderate correlation[a]		High correlation[a]	
σ_ω	σ_μ	High coeff.	Low coeff.	High coeff.	Low coeff.	High coeff.	Low coeff.	High coeff.	Low coeff.
	0.2	-0.05	-0.41	-0.10	-0.87	0.85	0.099	1.23	0.22
0.2	0.4	-0.09	-0.39	-0.17	-0.74	0.81	0.187	1.11	0.29
	0.5	-0.11	-0.36	-0.19	-0.73	0.81	0.279	1.06	0.34
	0.6	-0.14	-0.31	-0.23	-0.65	0.81	0.325	1.01	0.37
	0.2	-0.05	-0.42	-0.08	-0.95	1.09	0.111	1.53	0.15
0.4	0.4	-0.08	-0.45	-0.14	-0.92	1.02	0.165	1.40	0.30
	0.5	-0.10	-0.40	-0.20	-0.81	0.99	0.249	1.28	0.31
	0.6	-0.12	-0.37	-0.18	-0.84	1.05	0.288	1.25	0.33

[a]Correlation refers to correlation between leader effects, YA, and constituency characteristics, Z.

The comparison between the estimated and actual coefficients can be explored further by computing the simple correlations between the average estimated coefficients in each simulation and the true values of these coefficients. These correlations are shown in Table A.9. They are quite high. The lowest correlation among the leader coefficients is 0.94, and most are on the order of 0.97. The lowest of the correlations among the constituency coefficients is 0.86 and most are larger than 0.90. The only noticeable pattern is that the leader correlations are lower in the simulations with a high correlation between leadership effects and constituency demographic variables, while the correlations for the constituency coefficients are higher. The correlations suggest that even though there are biases to the coefficient estimates, they do reflect the pattern of influence or relative importance of the different variables.

The statistical inferences made about the true values of the

TABLE A.9. CORRELATIONS BETWEEN ACTUAL AND ESTIMATED COEFFICIENTS

Error term standard deviations		Leader coefficients		Constituency coefficients	
σ_ω	σ_μ	Moderate correlation[a]	High correlation[a]	Moderate correlation[a]	High correlation[a]
	0.2	0.96	0.95	0.90	0.98
	0.4	0.97	0.95	0.88	0.94
0.2	0.5	0.97	0.95	0.88	0.93
	0.6	0.96	0.95	0.86	0.92
	0.2	0.96	0.94	0.90	0.97
	0.4	0.98	0.95	0.91	0.96
0.4	0.5	0.98	0.96	0.90	0.93
	0.6	0.96	0.95	0.87	0.95

[a]Correlation refers to correlation between leader effects, YA, and constituency characteristics, Z.

coefficients and about which influences are important can also be examined. These inferences are made using the estimated standard errors of each coefficient and a critical value of 5 percent. This evaluation is important because much of the discussion in Chapters 4 and 5 is based on conclusions about which variables were influential and which ones were not. Consequently, it is important to know how reliable these conclusions are. There are two types of problems. The null hypothesis of no influence can either be falsely rejected, a type I error, or it could be falsely accepted, a type II error. In the former case, the error leads to the mistaken conclusion that an unimportant variable does exert some influence, while in the latter, an error results in the erroneous conclusion that an important variable has no influence. The statistical test being used is geared to limiting the occurrence of the first type of error, although one must be cautious of the second type as well.

The results of these tests, shown in Table A.10, indicate that type II errors are made less frequently than type I errors. The only exception is the constituency variable in the simulations with a large variance in the constituency opinion model and a small correlation between the leadership effects and the constituency demographic variables. Furthermore, the type II errors are more likely to occur with the constituency than with the leader variable. There are consistently more type II constituency errors than leadership errors in the simulations with a small association between the leader effects and the constituency variables. In the case of a high correlation between these variables, the type II problems become apparent in the leader coefficients only as the variance in the voting models, σ_u, increases. This means that in a majority of the simulations there is less likelihood of mistakenly inferring that leaders are unimportant than of inferring that constituency is unimportant.

Type I errors are more frequent than type II errors except in the four simulations noted above. In a majority of simulations the type I errors are more prevalent among the leader coefficients. For

TABLE A.10. HYPOTHESIS TESTS

Error term standard deviations		Leader coefficients				Constituency coefficient			
		Moderate correlation[a]		High correlation[a]		Moderate correlation[a]		High correlation[a]	
σ_ω	σ_μ	Type II error	Type I error	Type II error	Type I error	Type II error	Type I error	Type II error	Type I error
	0.2	0	65	0	182	4	47	0	61
	0.4	4	51	25	161	12	45	4	58
0.2	0.5	10	53	36	144	15	52	3	64(1)[b]
	0.6	28	42	63	113	31	52(2)	13	58(1)
	0.2	0	36	0	109	42	28	22	46(3)
	0.4	1	33	12	100	60	41	28	48
0.4	0.5	10	32	39	83	61	46(2)	28	49
	0.6	25	27	47	84	67	44	28	62

[a]Correlation refers to correlation between leader effects, YA, and constituency characteristics, Z.

[b]Parentheses indicate number of cases where null hypothesis was reflected in favor of a conclusion that constituency had a negative influence. All the other Type I constituency errors led to the conclusion that constituency had a positive influence. All the Type I errors led to the conclusion that the leader coefficient was negative.

172

the leader coefficients, these errors always mistakenly infer that a leader has a negative influence on a legislator's position when no influence actually exists. The interesting observation at this point, however, is that there are very few estimated negative leadership coefficients in the results in Chapter 4. This may indicate that type I problems occurred infrequently in the actual estimations. The type I errors for the constituency coefficients consist of the erroneous inference that constituency has a positive influence. In only nine cases is constituency mistaken to have a negative influence when in fact none exists. These simulated results indicate that the procedures followed are more likely to lead to erroneous inferences about the constituency coefficients than about the leadership coefficients, and that in most cases the erroneous inference would be that constituency is important when it is not. Thus, there seems to be a tendency to overstate the importance of constituency.

An exception to this conclusion is the simulation which may best represent the real world. This is the simulation with large variances in the constituency opinion model and only moderate associations between leadership effects and the demographic variables. There were many nonsouthern states with both a Democratic and a Republican senator, which would reduce the amount of correlation between the demographic variables and the leadership effects and suggest that the simulations with moderate correlations between these two factors may be more appropriate. In these simulations, more errors are made in the inferences about the constituency coefficients, and a majority of these errors are inferences that constituency is not important.

The final comparisons concern the average fits of the estimated models under the different situations. Table A.11 shows these average fits as measured by the average R^2 for each estimation. The average fits are shown separately for legislators with low and high constituency coefficients. The fits are consistently higher for legislators with low constituency coefficients. For legislators with high constituency coefficients, the fits are higher in the

TABLE A.11. AVERAGE FITS

Error term standard deviations		Moderate correlation[a]		High correlation[a]	
σ_ω	σ_μ	Low coeff.	High coeff.	Low coeff.	High coeff.
	0.2	0.91	0.52	0.92	0.70
	0.4	0.74	0.47	0.76	0.61
0.2	0.5	0.68	0.45	0.69	0.56
	0.6	0.61	0.42	0.62	0.52
	0.2	0.89	0.40	0.90	0.49
	0.4	0.75	0.37	0.74	0.45
0.4	0.5	0.67	0.36	0.67	0.43
	0.6	0.59	0.36	0.61	0.43

[a]Correlation refers to correlation between leader effects, YA, and constituency characteristics, Z.

simulations with higher correlations between the leadership effects and the demographic variables, while for the legislators with low constituency coefficients this association does not have a noticeable effect on the fits. In all cases, the fits decrease as the variances in the voting models increase, and only in the case of the legislators with high constituency coefficients do the fits decrease with increased variances in the constituency opinion models. The conclusion here is that the observed fits do vary with the amount of the variance in each legislator's voting model. This is important because most of the analysis in Chapter 6 is based on the fits for different groups of senators on the different issues. The assumption there is that the residuals in the estimated models reflect deviations in senators' voting behavior from their systematic patterns. These deviations are then used to try to infer some causes, such as logrolling. Since the simulations imply that the fits of the estimated models do vary systematically with the amount of deviation in legislators' voting behavior, there is a greater likelihood that the deviations discussed in Chapter 6 do reflect deviations in the senators' voting patterns.

CONCLUSION

This appendix illustrates the difficulties inherent in obtaining the appropriate variables to estimate models of legislative behavior. The analysis of the 1970 senate defeat of the Family Assistance Plan, comparing a constituency variable obtained from survey data with a variable developed from the association between senators' votes and the characteristics of their state's population, as is done in this study, indicates a substantial correlation between the two measures. It is quite possible that the discrepancy between the two variables results because neither is a perfect measure of constituency opinion and both contain some measurement error, which differs in each variable. The analytical and simulation analyses of the constituency variable used here do indicate that the errors in that variable are not random, however, but are associated with both the true constituency and leadership variables. The difficulty with these systematic errors is that they lead to overestimates of the importance of constituency influences and understatement of leaders' influences. Fortunately, the simulation study also indicates that in spite of the biases the estimated and actual equations are probably highly correlated, providing additional justification for the procedure.

MATHEMATICAL NOTE

This note derives some of the statistical properties of the simple statistical model shown in Eq. A.7. The estimates of the coefficients in a senator's model, A_j and C_j, will be unbiased only if the error term, $(U_j + e_j C_j)$ is independent of X_j and Y. In other words, if

(A.8) $E[\hat{X}_j{}' (U_j + e_j C_j)] = E[\hat{X}_j{}' (U_j + C_j X_j - C_j \hat{X}_j)] = 0$, and

(A.9) $E[Y'(U_j + e_j C_j)] = E[Y'(U_j + C_j X_j - C_j \hat{X}_j)] = 0.$

Expanding Eq. A.8 and using Eqs. A.2 and A.6, gives

$$E\left\{ Z_j'(ZZ')^{-1}Z(A'Y' + CX' + U')[U_j + C_j X_j - C_j(YA + XC + U) \right.$$
$$\left. Z'(ZZ')^{-1}Z_j] \right\} = Z_j'(ZZ')^{-1}Z\left\{ (A'Y' + CX')E(U_j) + E(U'U_j) + A'Y'C_j X_j \right.$$
$$+ CX'C_j X_j + E(U')C_j X_j$$
$$- C_j(A'Y' + CX')(YA + XC)Z'(ZZ')^{-1}Z_j$$
$$- C_j[E(U')(YA + XC) + (A'Y' + CX')E(U)]\,Z'(ZZ')^{-1}Z_j$$
$$\left. - C_j E(U'U)Z'(ZZ')^{-1}Z_j \right\}.$$

This can be written as

(A.10) $Z_j'(ZZ')^{-1}Z\left\{ E(U'U_j) - C_j E(U'U)Z'(ZZ')^{-1}Z_j + E[C_j A'Y'X_j \right.$
$$\left. + C_j CX'X_j - C_j(A'Y' + CX')(YA + XC)Z'(ZZ')^{-1}Z_j] \right\},$$

since $E(U)$ and $E(U_j) = 0$ and C_j is a scalar value. If the error terms in all senators models are assumed to have the same variance and are independent of each other, then

$$E(U'U_j) = \begin{bmatrix} 0 \\ 0 \\ \vdots \\ M\sigma_u^2 \\ \vdots \\ 0 \end{bmatrix}$$

and $E(U'U) = M\sigma_u^2 I$

where M is the number of bills in the sample. The first part of Exp. A.10 can then be written as

$$
Z_j{}'(ZZ')^{-1}Z \left[\begin{bmatrix} 0 \\ \vdots \\ M\sigma_u^2 \\ 0 \\ \vdots \\ 0 \end{bmatrix} - C_j M\sigma_u^2\, Z'(ZZ')^{-1}Z_j \right] = Z_j{}'(ZZ')^{-1}Z
$$

$$
\begin{bmatrix} 0 \\ \vdots \\ M\sigma_u^2 \\ \vdots \\ u \end{bmatrix} - Z_j{}'(ZZ')^{-1}ZC_jM\sigma_u^2\, Z'(ZZ')^{-1}Z_j)
$$

$$
= Z_j{}'(ZZ')^{-1}Z_j M\sigma_u^2 - C_j M\sigma_u^2\, Z_j{}'(ZZ')^{-1}Z_j
$$
$$
= M\sigma_u^2\, Z_j{}'(ZZ')^{-1}Z_j\,(1 - C_j).
$$

Thus, the first part of this expression will equal 0 only if C_j equals 1 and if C_j is less than 1 it increases as σ_u^2 increases. The second part of Exp. A.10 equals

$$
C_j Z_j{}'(ZZ')^{-1}Z\, E[A'Y'X_j + CX'X_j - (A'Y'YA + A'Y'XC + CX'YA + CX'XC)Z'(ZZ')^{-1}Z_j].
$$

Using the assumption that $X = BZ + W$, this can be rewritten as

$$
C_j Z_j{}'(ZZ')^{-1}Z\, E[A'Y'(BZ_j + W_j) + C(Z'B' + W')\,(BZ_j + W_j)
$$
$$
- A'Y'(YA + BZC + WC)Z'(ZZ')^{-1}Z_j - C(Z'B' + W')YAZ'(ZZ')^{-1}Z_j
$$
$$
- C(Z'B' + W')\,(BZ + W)CZ'(ZZ')^{-1}Z_j].
$$

Assuming that $E(W) = 0$, this becomes

$$C_j Z_j'(ZZ')^{-1} Z[A'Y'BZ_j + CZ'B'BZ_j + CE(W'W_j) - A'Y'(YA$$
$$+ BZC)Z'(ZZ')^{-1}Z_j$$
$$-CZ'B'YAZ'(ZZ')^{-1}Z_j - CZ'B'BZCZ'(ZZ')^{-1}Z_j$$
$$-CE(W'W)C Z'(ZZ')^{-1}Z_j$$
$$= C_j Z_j'(ZZ')^{-1} Z \left\{ A'Y' [BZ_j - (YA + BZC)Z'(ZZ')^{-1}Z_j] \right.$$
$$+ CZ'B' [BZ_j - (YA + BZC)Z'(ZZ')^{-1}Z_j]$$
$$\left. + C[E(W'W_j) - E(W'W)CZ'(ZZ')^{-1}Z_j] \right\}.$$

If $E(W'W) = N\sigma_w^2 \, I$, then this expression equals

$$(A.11) \quad C_j Z_j(ZZ')^{-1} Z (A'Y' + CZ'B') [BZ_j - (YA + BZC)Z'(ZZ')^{-1}Z_j]$$

$$+ C_j Z_j'(ZZ')^{-1}ZC \begin{bmatrix} 0 \\ \vdots \\ N\sigma_w^2 \\ \vdots \\ 0 \end{bmatrix} - C_j Z_j'(ZZ')^{-1} ZC(N\sigma_w^2)CZ'(ZZ')^{-1}Z_j.$$

If $C_j = 0$, then this expression equals 0, and the bias is only related to σ_u^2. If all the legislators have constituency coefficients equal to 1, $C = I$, and the leadership effects, YA, are uncorrelated with the demographic variables, $YAZ' = 0$, then the expression in Exp. A.11 will equal 0. If both these conditions hold, then Exp. A.11 reduces to

$$(A.12) \quad Z_j'(ZZ')^{-1}Z(YA + BZ)' [BZ_j - YAZ'(ZZ')^{-1}Z_j - BZZ'(ZZ')^{-1}Z_j]$$
$$+ Z_j'(ZZ')^{-1}Z_j N\sigma_w^2 - Z_j'(ZZ')^{-1}Z_j N\sigma_w^2.$$

This expression equals zero, since $BZ_j - BZ_j = YAZ' = 0$ by assumption.

This analysis implies there are three conditions which will affect the estimates of the coefficients in each senators model. The first is the variance of the error terms in each senators voting model. The larger this variance, the higher the correlation between the error term in Eq. A.7 and the variable $\hat{X}_j$. The second condition is the extent to which senators' constituency coefficients differ from the value 1. This is represented by the expression $C = I$. The final condition, written as $YAZ' = 0$, is the extent to which the leadership effects in each bill, YA, are correlated with the demographic variables describing each constituency, Z. Unfortunately, the expressions involving each of these conditions are too complicated to permit an easy evaluation of the consequences of not meeting them. It is also quite apparent that none of these conditions will be met in any real legislature. The question of how serious deviations from these conditions might be is difficult to answer but is explored in the simulation of these techniques.

The expression for the bias of the leadership coefficients is simpler. In the case of Eq. A.9

$$(A.13) \quad E[Y'(U_j + C_j X_j - C_j \hat{X}_j)]$$

$$= Y'E(U_j) + E[C_j Y'X_j] - C_j Y'E(\hat{X}_j)$$

$$= E(C_j Y'X_j) - C_j Y'E[(YA + XC + U)\,Z'(ZZ')^{-1}Z_j]$$

$$= C_j Y'[BZ_j + E(W_j)] - C_j Y'[(YA + BZC + E(W)C + E(U)]$$
$$Z'(ZZ')^{-1}Z_j$$

$$= C_j Y'[BZ_j - BZCZ'(ZZ')^{-1}Z_j - YAZ'(ZZ')^{-1}Z_j.$$

Again, Eq. A.13 will only equal 0 if $C = I$ and $YAZ' = 0$, or if $C_j = 0$.

The conditions that affect the estimates of constituency influence also determine the bias to the leader coefficients with the exception of the term involving U. These conditions are the extent to which senators' constituency coefficients deviate from the value one, $C = I$, or zero, $C_j = 0$, and the systematic relationship between leadership effects, YA, and the demographic variables describing each constituency, Z. The effect on the leadership coefficients of not meeting these conditions is again explored with the monte carlo simulation of the estimating procedures.

NOTES

1. A more detailed study of senators' votes on the FAP issue and their relationship to constituency positions is contained in Otto A. Davis and John E. Jackson, "Senate Defeat of the Family Assistance Plan," *Public Policy*, vol. 22, no. 3 (Summer, 1974).

2. The coefficient of reproducibility is 0.976 and the minimal margin reproducibility is 0.729.

3. The precise formulation of the constituency variable is shown below. Consider the following definitions:

$F_{i,j,k}^{w}$ = proportion of metropolitan ($i = 1$) or rural ($i = 2$) whites in income class j and region k who favor FAP from Table A.2;

$Y_{i,j,m}^{w}$ = proportion of metropolitan or nonmetropolitan whites in income class j in state m (which is in region k);

$N_{i,m}^{w}$ = number of whites in state m who live in metropolitan or non-metropolitan areas;

$F_{i,k}^{B}$ = proportion of metropolitan or nonmetropolitan nonwhites in region k who favor FAP, from Table A.2;

$N_{i,m}^{B}$ = number of nonwhites in area i and state m (in region k); and

N_{m} = total population in state $m = N_{1,m}^{w} + N_{2,m}^{w} + N_{1,m}^{B} + N_{2,m}^{B}$.

These definitions, the income distribution data estimated by the method outlined above, the number of whites and nonwhites in metropolitan and nonmetropolitan areas in each state, and the proportion of each group expected to favor a Family Assistance Plan from Table A.2, can be used to estimated the proportion of each state's population favoring FAP (denoted by C_{m}) by the following formulation:

$$C_m = \left[\sum_{j=1}^{6} (F_{1,j,k}^{w} * Y_{1,j,m}^{w} * N_{1,m}^{w}) + \sum_{j=1}^{6} (F_{2,j,k}^{w} * Y_{2,j,m}^{w} * N_{2,m}^{w}) + F_{1,k}^{B} * N_{1,m}^{B} + F_{2,k}^{B} * N_{2,m}^{B} \right] / (N_m).$$

4. The procedure used to estimate this equation was one developed specially for Guttman scales. See William Zavoina and Richard McKelvey, "A Statistical Model for the Analysis of Legislative Voting Behavior," paper presented at the Annual Meeting of the American Political Science Association, September 1–6, 1969, New York, N.Y. Appendix B contains an ex-

tended treatment of the problems of using Guttman scale scores as the dependent variable in a regression analysis.

5. An estimation using an alternative constituency variable also derived from the SRC survey implied that southern Democrats gave even less weight to nonwhites than that shown in Table A.3. See Davis and Jackson, "Represenative Assemblies."

6. See note 9, Chapter 3.

7. The development of the simulation was aided considerably by comments from Harold W. Stanley, "Estimating Parameters in Roll Call Voting: A Preliminary Investigation of Possible Bias in the Jackson Method," paper prepared for PLSC 73b, Professors Kramer and Berman, Yale University, June 9, 1972.

Appendix B. Problems of Guttman Scaling, Functional Form, and Coefficient Estimation

Linear regression analysis is used to estimate the weights senators gave their constituencies and various leader and colleague variables in deciding how much support to give each bill. However, linear regression contains the implicit assumption that the scale scores measuring senators' support for each bill constitute an interval variable. This assumption is clearly inappropriate for variables developed from Guttman scales, which only provide a highly aggregated ordinal measure of senators' support for each bill. The question then is, how much were the results affected by making this assumption? This appendix explores an answer by postulating an alternative stochastic model to explain a senator's support for each bill and uses a different statistical procedure to estimate the influence of the hypothesized variables.

The alternative model examined is the limited dependent variable (LDV) or "probit" regression model developed by Tobin.[1] Although the model still requires some assumptions that are not met by the Guttman scale variables, it does account for one of the most serious violations of linear regression. Thus, it should provide at least partial evidence about how much the previous results are affected by the use of ordinary least squares.

THE DIFFICULTIES WITH GUTTMAN VARIABLES

There is an inherent difficulty in the use of Guttman scales. To illustrate, consider Fig. B.1, in which the line $Y^* = a + bX$ purports to represent the expected relationship between Y (senators' preferences) and X (their constituencies' preferences). More precisely, allowing for stochastic disturbances, the line represents the expected preferences of a senator given a value for X, that is, $E(Y|X) = a + bX$. Their actual preferences, if they could be ascertained, would deviate randomly about the line and are represented by the equation $Y = a + bX + e$, where e represents the random deviations. In this case, the ordinary least squares regression of Y on X would give unbiased estimates of the coefficients a and b since the values of the regressor X and the disturbance e are uncorrelated.

However, in the case of senate voting, the only way to measure senators' positions on a bill, and hence Y, is by their votes on the various amendments. The Guttman scale combines these votes into a scalar measure. But it is clear that this measure offers only a distorted picture of Y. The dotted lines in Fig. B.1 show where four different amendments might have been located on this underlying continuous dimension. For the Civil Rights Commis-

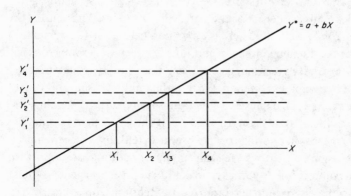

FIGURE B.1.

sion, illustrated in Chapter 3, the attempt to prevent the senate from considering any extension corresponds to Y'_1, the two-year extension to Y'_2, the four-year extension to Y'_3, and establishing a permanent agency to Y'_4. The Guttman procedure then assigns a score of 0 to those senators who voted against all four amendments. Senators who voted for the weakest amendment, Y'_1 but for no others are assigned to the second group with a value of 1. And so on, with the senators who voted for all the amendments assigned a value of 4. The distortion arises because all senators with the same scale score are taken to have identical positions, when in fact they may differ by as much as the distance between the appropriate two amendments. In the case of the Civil Rights Commission, for example, senators preferring either a 2, 2.5, 3 or 3.9 year extension are all scored a 2, and all senators who want at least a four-year but less than a permanent extension are scored a 3. Due to the aggregation, each Guttman score contains an additional error component to the previously discussed stochastic disturbance. The problems created by this aggregation process are most severe for extreme values of X and will be discussed separately.

The Civil Rights Commission scale can be used to illustrate a second problem inherent in the use of Guttman scale scores as measures of senators' preferences. The Guttman scale only provides a rank ordering of the votes on a given bill, and thus of the senators' positions. There is no way to determine the "distance" between the amendments, and thus between the groups of senators on the underlying dimension. Using the scale scores as variables in a linear regression model makes the implicit assumption that the ranks approximately reflect the spacing of the amendments along the Y dimension. In the case of the Civil Rights Commission, this means that voting for a two-year extension rather than no extension constitutes the same amount of additional support for the commission as voting to make it a permanent agency rather than merely permitting a four-year extension. This is clearly a strong assumption, particularly on bills where the underlying dimension is not as clear.

The most serious problem created by the use of Guttman scale scores in linear regression, however, is the systematic correlation introduced between the explanatory variables and the deviations about both the senators' expected preference, Y^*, and their expected scale score. In Figure B.2, let the line $Y^* = a + bX$ again be the senators' expected preferences given X, let Y^{**} be the line representing the expected Guttman scale scores for each value of X, and let Y_j be the actual preferences of senators given by $Y_j = a + bX + e_j$, where the e_j are different possible error terms. There are two different systematic errors. The first is introduced by trying to approximate the line Y^* by the step function Y^{**}. For extreme values of X, and hence of Y, the step function ceases to discriminate among senators with extreme preferences. This error, defined as $Y^* - Y^{**}$, is largest for values of X less than X_1 and greater than X_4, and is negative for small values of X and positive for large values. This introduces a systematic correlation between the errors and X. If the amendments offered to most bills adequately covered the range of senators'

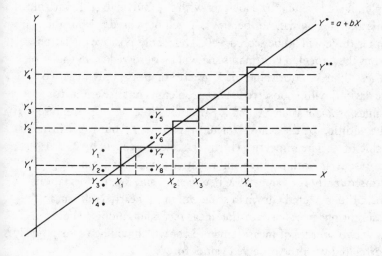

FIGURE B.2.

preferences, this would not cause much of a problem because there would be few senators in each of these tails. Unfortunately, the senate does not spend much time considering extreme amendments, so that on many bills these areas are likely to contain a significant number of senators with different preferences and different values of X. Or, worse, senators may be located in one of the tails on a large number of bills. In this case, they may be following their constituencies' preferences, but that will not be reflected in the Guttman scale scores because they will be scored a 0 or a 4 on most bills, and the linear regression model will seriously underestimate the coefficients in the senators' models.

A second problem is the nature of the deviations about the expected Guttman scale scores, Y^{**}. For X less than X_1 only positive deviations from expected Guttman scale score, which is itself an erroneous estimate of Y^*, will be observed. For example, Y_1 and Y_2 represent the presence of two different positive error terms, while Y_3 and Y_4 are the result of two negative error terms of the same magnitudes. In the linear regression model, using a continuous dependent variable to estimate $Y^* = a + bX$, this pattern would satisfy the basic assumption of an error term with an expected value of 0. However with the Guttman scale variable, this assumption will not be met, Y_1 will be scored a 1 but the other three will all be scored as 0. Thus, only positive deviations from the expected Guttman scale will be observed from values of X less than X_1. For values of X greater than X_4, only negative deviations will be observed. This problem is not as serious for values of X between X_1 and X_4. For example, $Y_5 - Y_8$ represent the addition of the same error terms as $Y_1 - Y_4$ but for a different value of X. The respective Guttman scale scores will be 2, 1, 1, 0, representing both positive and negative deviations from Y^{**}. Consequently for values of X between X_1 and X_4, the deviations from the expected Guttman scale will more nearly conform to the assumptions necessary for the linear regression model. There are now two sources of measurement error which will be systematically correlated with the observed values for X.

Both problems arise from the limited range of the amendments offered to each bill and have the same implications for the use of the Guttman scale scores as dependent variables in a linear regression. Due both to the inability of the step function Y^{**} to approximate the line Y^* for extreme values of X and to the systematic exclusion of negative error terms for X less than X_1 and positive error terms for X greater than X_4, small values of X are associated with positive error terms in the Guttman scale data, and large values of X are associated with negative error terms. This leads to a negative correlation between the error term and the explanatory variable. (If the effect of X on Y had been negative, for example, $Y^* = a - bX$, then there would have been a positive correlation between X and the expected value of the error term.) Thus, the ordinary least squares estimation using the Guttman scale scores does not satisfy the necessary assumptions of linear regression and will not yield the same results as a model estimating Y^* if the actual values for Y could be observed. These violations of the assumptions may result in an underestimation of the true value of b, as the fitted line attempts to fit Y^{**} rather than Y^*.

ESTIMATIONS USING GUTTMAN SCALES AS A LIMITED DEPENDENT VARIABLE

Zavoina and McKelvey propose an alternative model which they call n-chotomous multivariate probit analysis.[2] It is an extension of probit analysis to the case where there are n rather than just two groupings of the dependent variable. Their program uses a maximum likelihood procedure to estimate both the coefficients in the underlying multivariate model and the location of the $(n - 1)$ dividing points used to construct the Guttman scale. The assumptions required for the n-chotomous procedure are that the senators' expected preferences are a linear function of the explanatory variables, $Y^* = \Sigma B_k X_k$, and the error term between this and their actual preferences on any bill, given by $Y_j = B_k X_k + e_j$, is normally distributed with mean zero and constant variance, and the $(n - 1)$ dividing points used in the scaling procedure have aggregated this behavior into n ordinal categories, or groups.

The limited dependent variable technique to be used in this paper represents a compromise between OLS and n-chotomous probit analysis. The LDV model permits the measured dependent variable to be grouped at one end of the underlying dimension. This grouping then forms a limit value for the dependent variable. The dependent variable is assumed to be an interval, continuous variable and a linear function of the explanatory variables at all points above this limit.

This limited dependent variable model is shown in Fig. B.3, represented by the line W. The model shows that if the limit is a lower bound, the measured value of Y cannot be less than the limit, no matter how much less than X_1, X might be, or how large a negative stochastic disturbance might be included in the senator's actual preference for that observation. Suppose for reasons of constituency preference or purely random circumstances senators are willing to vote for more restrictive amendments than Y'_1. The

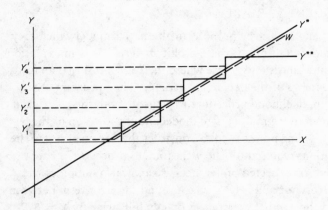

FIGURE B.3.

LDV model in effect gives them a latent score of -1 or even a -2, even though this is not manifest in the values of Y. (The same description holds, only in reverse, if the limit is an upper bound. Even though a senator might be willing to vote for stronger legislation than Y_4', he cannot be scored higher than 4.) At all other points, W is assumed to follow the linear model of Y^* with an error term. The LDV model, with a lower bound, is:

$$(1) \qquad E(Y|X) = Y^* = B_0 + B_1 X_1 + \ldots B_k X_k$$

$$(2) \qquad W = \begin{cases} L & \text{if } Y^* < L \\ Y^* & \text{if } Y^* \geqslant L \end{cases}$$

Where W is the limited dependent variable, Y^* is the expected preference and is a linear function of the explanatory variables. The parameters of the LDV model are estimated by maximum likelihood, given observations on $Y, X_1, \ldots,$ and X_k.

For Guttman scale purposes, LDV represents a compromise between the linear regression model and the Zavoina-McKelvey approach. In the LDV model, the dependent variable, once it passes the limit, is assumed to be an interval and unbounded variable. This is not the case with Guttman scales so that the problems pointed out by Zavoina and McKelvey will still exist at these nonlimit points. In terms of Figure B.3, LDV will not do justice to Y^{**}, but will at least do justice to the threshold. However, the advantages of n-chotomous probit over LDV should decrease as the number of groupings increases and as the number of extreme observations becomes concentrated at one end, rather than at both ends, of the scale. Thus, both LDV and OLS would become more appropriate as the number of amendments included, that is, the number of dividing points, increases, and LDV would become more appropriate as the number of limit observations becomes concentrated at one of the limits.

The problem now is one of selecting an estimating procedure for the senators' voting models and the variables constructed from

Guttman scales. The advantages of linear regression are that it is readily available, inexpensive, has shown considerable robustness in the face of real world problems, and is the best understood technique. The assumptions of the n-chotomous procedure, on the other hand, better satisfy the model and type of data at hand. However, it is not readily available in programmed form, most readers will not be acquainted with the technique, its robustness is unknown, and it is more expensive computationally. Probit regression appears to occupy a middle position in these considerations. The data at hand satisfy the LDV assumptions better than the linear regression assumptions, but possibly not as well as those of n-chotomous probit. LDV is not as widely used or understood as OLS among social scientists but is better known than n-chotomous probit.

When the study of senate voting behavior was initiated, linear regression was selected because of its availability, computational efficiency, robustness, and familiarity, and in spite of its inappropriate assumptions. Now that alternative models are feasible, the question arises whether the results and conclusions about senate voting behavior would have been different had a more appropriate technique been used.[3]

LIMITED DEPENDENT VARIABLE ESTIMATE OF SENATORS' VOTING BEHAVIOR

We now turn to an examination of the limited dependent variable models and their results. The question of whether senators' voting behavior is better approximated by a LDV model with an upper or lower limit is quite easy to answer. The senators with many limit values generally had them concentrated at one limit. Table B.1 shows the distribution of senators by the number of observations at their less frequently observed limit. For example, if a senator is scored as 4 on twenty bills and 0 on only three bills, he appears under the 3 column in Table B.1. This should support the statement that most senators have very few observations at both limits and that they conform to the LDV model.

TABLE B.1. FREQUENCY OF THE LESS-FREQUENT
LIMIT OBSERVATIONS

Number of less-frequent limit observations	0	1	2	3	4	5	6	7	8	9	10
Number of senators	17	28	19	11	8	9	1	4	2	1	1

Each of the 101 senators' models is reestimated using the LDV procedure. The results are compared with the linear regression results on three criteria. The first is the goodness of fit to the 1961–62 data used to estimate the models. The second concerns the number of times the null hypothesis of no systematic influence by an explanatory variable is rejected. The third criterion is the ability to predict the senators' voting scale scores on twenty-five bills in the 1963 session.

The estimated scores for the linear regression are the calculated values of Y from the OLS-estimated regression, $\hat{Y}$, denoted subsequently as Y^1. The LDV predictions, denoted as Y^2, are the calculated expected values from the maximum likelihood estimated LDV model:

$$\text{(B.3)} \quad \hat{Y}_2 = L \left[\hat{P}_r \left(Y < L \right) \right] + \int_L^\infty v \left[\hat{P}_r \left(Y = v \right) \right] dv.$$

Where $\hat{P}_r \left(Y < L \right)$ is the estimated probability that the senator's preference is less than the limit L, and $\hat{P}_r \left(Y = v \right)$ is the estimated probability that the senator's preference equals v. These estimated probabilities are calculated from the senator's expected preference, Y^*, shown in equation B.1 and from the assumption that actual preferences are normally distributed around Y^* with some variance σ^2, which is estimated by the LDV procedure.

The estimated scores are then compared with the observed scores. The prediction or postdiction errors for the ith senator on bill j are $U_i^1(j) = [Y_i(j) - Y_i^1(j)]$ and $U_i^2(j) = [Y_i(j) - Y_i^2(j)]$

respectively. The errors for each model are then squared and
summed for each bill and for each senator, and the mean squared
errors are computed. The mean squared errors will form the basis
for our comparisons of the two alternative statistical models.

Postdicting 1961–1962

Table B.2 shows the distribution of the differences obtained
by subtracting the LDV mean squared error from the OLS mean
squared error for each of the 101 senators. The LDV procedure
has a lower mean squared error for slightly more than half the
senators, 54 out of 101. In 24 of the 35 cases where the magnitude
of the absolute difference exceeds 0.05, it is LDV that has the
smaller mean squared error.

When related to the size of the mean squared error, the absolute
differences are very small. The ratio of the absolute difference in
mean squared errors to the ordinary least squares mean squared
errors is computed for each senator. This ratio was less than 0.10
for nearly 60 percent of the senators. It exceeds 0.30 for only 8
senators, and most of these have very small mean squared errors.

A similar comparison may be made across bills, rather than
across senators. Table B.3 gives the results. The LDV procedure
out-performs OLS on this criterion for slightly more than half the
bills, 20 out of 36. Again, the differences between the two
methods are not substantial. Thus, in terms of goodness of fit
over the sample, LDV is only slightly better than linear regression.

Significance of Explanatory Variables

The second comparison concerns the explanatory variables
found nonsignificant (at the 5 percent level) by the two procedures.
This comparison is made to see if the two techniques lead to con-
tradictory conclusions about the influence of the different variables hypothesized to affect senate voting. For example, if the
LDV procedure accepts the null hypothesis of no influence by the
party floor leaders more often than OLS does, it raises doubts

TABLE B.2. OLS MEAN SQUARED ERROR MINUS LDV MEAN
SQUARED ERROR FOR SENATORS IN 1961–62

Difference	$\leqslant -0.100$	-0.050 -0.099	-0.000 -0.049	0.000 0.049	0.050 0.099	$\geqslant 0.100$
Number of senators	4	7	36	30	16	8

TABLE B.3. OLS MEAN SQUARED ERROR MINUS LDV MEAN
SQUARED ERROR FOR BILLS IN 1961–62

Difference	$\leqslant -0.100$	-0.050 -0.099	-0.000 -0.049	0.000 0.049	0.050 0.099	$\geqslant 0.100$
Number of bills	1	5	10	12	5	3

about the previous conclusion that Mansfield was an important
factor in how nonsouthern Democratic senators voted.

In the regression model, the significance test is made by assuming that the ratio of an estimated coefficient to its estimated
standard error is distributed as a t-statistic. The two-tailed test is
used. For the LDV model, the null hypothesis is tested by comparing the log of the likelihood function when the variable is
excluded to this value when the variable is included. Minus two
times this difference $(-2\ln\lambda)$ is assumed to be distributed as a
χ^2 with one degree of freedom.

The results of these calculations do not show any conflict
between the two techniques. They lead to different conclusions
with respect to only 26 of the over 600 coefficients estimated.
These differences involve the models of 23 senators. Ordinary
least squares leads to rejection of a null hypothesis accepted by
LDV in 13 cases and accepts a null hypothesis rejected by LDV
in 13 cases. Ordinary least squares rejects the null hypothesis of no
influence for the party leader (Mansfield or Dirksen) and other

senator (Morse in Gruening's model, for example) variables more often than LDV, while LDV rejects the null hypothesis of no influence more often for the constituency and committee liberal/conservative variables. These differences are quite small, however, never more than 2 or 3 for any variable.

These slight differences indicate that the two techniques yield the same conclusions about the significance of constituencies, party leaders, and the president. The conclusions reached previously are not essentially altered by using the LDV procedure rather than linear regression.

Prediction of 1963 Votes

The only consistent differences in the two procedures appear when the two models are used to predict voting behavior during the 1963 session of the senate. The differences between the observed scale scores and the predicted scale scores for each model are analyzed the same way as the differences from the 1961–1962 votes.

Figure B.4 shows a plot of the actual scale scores as a function of constituency for Senator Bartlett (D., Alaska) for the twenty-five bills in 1963. Also shown are lines representing the expected scale scores for these bills using the limited dependent variable and ordinary least squares models. Senator Bartlett is selected because since constituency is the only statistically significant variable in his model, it can be plotted in two dimensions. This case also provides an illustration of the use of the LDV model when there is an upper rather than a lower limit. It is fairly typical in terms of the goodness of fit to the 1963 data. This should help give a picture of these models and show what an average fit looks like for the 1963 observations.

Table B.4 shows the distribution of the differences obtained by subtracting the LDV mean squared error from the OLS mean squared error for each of the 86 senators in the 1963 sample. Two thirds of the senators (56 of 86) have lower mean squared errors

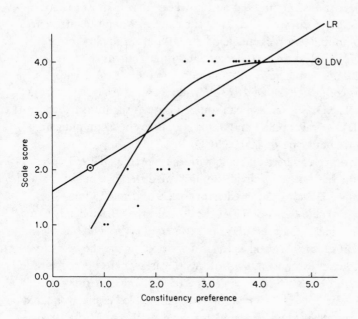

FIGURE B.4. Plot of Scale Score versus Constituency for Senator Bartlett, 1963 Bills

TABLE B.4. OLS MEAN SQUARED ERROR MINUS LDV MEAN SQUARED ERROR FOR SENATORS IN 1963

		-0.100	0.000	0.000	0.100	
Difference	≤ -0.200	-0.199	-0.099	0.099	0.199	≥ 0.200
Number of senators	12	8	36	23	4	3

with the ordinary least squares models than they do with the LDV models. OLS also has the smaller mean squared error on 12 of the 15 cases where the magnitude of the difference is greater than 0.200. It should be pointed out, however, that in most cases the sizes of these differences are not substantial. When the differences are computed as a percentage of the OLS mean squared error, half (46) are less than 10 percent and three fourths (67) are less than 20 percent. The average mean squared error for each procedure is computed for all 2073 individual voting scale scores from 1963. The OLS average mean squared error is slightly smaller than the LDV average, 0.833 and 0.884, respectively, again indicating a slightly better performance by OLS.

The other comparison made with these predicted 1963 votes is on the basis of the individual bills. The difference between the OLS and LDV mean squared error for each of the 25 bills is shown in Table B.5. For 19 of the 25 bills, the OLS mean squared error is smaller than the LDV mean squared error. The size of these differences, as well as the distribution, favors the ordinary least squares estimates. In 14 of the 16 cases where the magnitude of the absolute difference exceeds 0.05, OLS gives better estimates. Not only is OLS more likely to have a lower mean squared error, but when there are large differences, OLS is almost always the superior technique.

The overall conclusion is that based on 1963 predictive ability, the ordinary least squares procedure is slightly preferable to the limited dependent variable method. When these results are combined with the earlier results, which show very little difference

TABLE B.5. OLS MEAN SQUARED ERROR MINUS LDV MEAN SQUARED ERROR FOR BILLS IN 1963

		-0.050	-0.000	0.000	0.050	
Difference	$\leqslant -0.100$	-0.099	-0.049	0.049	0.099	$\geqslant 0.100$
Number of bills	5	9	5	4	1	1

between the fits of the OLS and LDV procedures to the data used to estimate the models or in the results of individual hypothesis tests, linear regression appears to be the better model. These results, when combined with ordinary least squares' advantages on the basis of computational efficiency, availability, and readers' familiarity, indicate that linear regression can be profitably used to test hypotheses which can only be represented by ordinal, Guttman type data.

CONCLUSION

The LDV model, which on *a priori* grounds seems to be more appropriate for analysis of senate voting behavior, does not yield results which are clearly superior to those obtained using linear regression. The two approaches give essentially the same fit to the sample data and the same picture of which variables are significant. But in postsample prediction, linear regression produces slightly better forecasts than LDV.

There are at least two possible interpretations of the findings that linear regression and limited-dependent-variable give similar results. One is that linear regression is sufficiently robust to handle ordinal variables, as produced by Guttman scaling. This should be of considerable encouragement to those social scientists forced to deal with ordinal or noninterval data. A contrary interpretation is that neither LDV nor linear regression is appropriate for data of this type: both their assumptions are too strong for Guttman data. The facts that the models estimated with both techniques could reasonably predict voting behavior outside the sample used to estimate the models and that the conclusions about the influence of constituency and the various senate leaders are consistent with prior opinions strongly suggest that the models and techniques have more substance than the second interpretation allows.

The decision about whether to believe the regression results and the empirical findings about senate voting behavior and the influence of party leaders, the president, and constituencies turns on which of the previous interpretations about the choice of technique one adopts. If the *a priori* arguments that LDV is more appropriate to this data and that it corrects many of the theoretical problems associated with OLS are accepted, the conclusions and interpretations of the OLS model should be accepted. The LDV models then provide further evidence and justification for these conclusions. However, those who believe neither technique to be appropriate and maintain that the techniques are too similar to provide independent confirmation, may continue to reject the empirical conclusions.

NOTES

1. James Tobin, "Estimation of Relationships for Limited Dependent Variables," *Econometrica*, 26 (Jan. 1958).

2. William Zavoina and Richard McKelvey, "A Statistical Model for the Analysis of Legislative Voting Behavior," paper presented at the Annual Meeting of The American Political Science Association, September, 1969, New York, N.Y.

3. Zavoina and McKelvey graciously made their program available. Unfortunately, it arrived too late to be adopted and used in the following comparisons. It is applied in Appendix A, with results not much different from the OLS estimates.

Notes

1. LEGISLATIVE BEHAVIOR AND THE DETERMINANTS OF PUBLIC POLICY

1. David B. Truman, *The Congressional Party* (New York: John Wiley and Sons, 1959), particularly chaps. 4 and 6, and Donald R. Matthews, *U.S. Senators and Their World* (Chapel Hill: University of North Carolina Press, 1960).

2. Truman, *Congressional Party*, chap. 4, and Matthews, *U.S. Senators*, chap. 6.

3. Truman, *Congressional Party*, p. 133.

4. *Ibid.*, pp. 144 and 285.

5. William S. White, *Citadel: The Story of the U.S. Senate* (New York: Harper, 1957), and Joseph S. Clark et al., *The Senate Establishment* (New York: Hill and Wang, 1963). See also James MacGregor Burns, *The Deadlock of Democracy* (Englewood Cliffs, N.J.: Prentice-Hall, 1963).

6. Clark, *Senate Establishment*, pp. 99–103.

7. See White, *Citadel*, p. 87, for a description of how "bleak and languid frowns" from the Senate patriarchs killed a piece of legislation on which "they felt they had been inadequately consulted."

8. Donald R. Matthews and James A. Stimpson, "Decision-Making by U.S. Representatives: A Preliminary Model," paper presented at the Conference on Political Decision-Making, University of Kentucky, Lexington, Ky., April 10–11, 1968.

9. Lewis A. Froman, Jr., *Congressmen and Their Constituencies* (Chicago: Rand McNally, 1963), chap. 1.

10. This is the behavior implied by many models, both theoretical and empirical. See Duncan MacRae, *Dimensions of Congressmen Voting* (Berkeley: University of California Press, 1958), appendix C; Anthony Downs, *An Economic Theory of Democracy* (New York: Harper, 1958), p. 54 (although Downs subsequently considers a more complicated model); and O. A. Davis, Melvin J. Hinich, and Peter C. Ordeshook, "An Expository Development of a Mathematical Model of the Electoral," *American Political Science Review*, vol. 64, no. 2 (June 1970).

11. Downs, *Economic Theory*, pp. 55–60 and 67; John E. Jackson, "Intensities, Preferences, and Electoral Politics," *Social Science Research*, vol. 2, no. 3 (Fall 1973).

12. See Jackson, "Intensities," for an example of varying levels of concern and their association with policy preferences from the 1968 presidential election.

13. See John E. Jackson, "The Importance of Issues and Issue Importance in Presidential Elections," Program on Quantitative Analysis in Political Science, Discussion Paper #3, Government Department Data Center, Harvard University, Cambridge, Mass. (August 1972), for empirical evidence of this voting process at the presidential level.

14. See Downs, *Economic Theory*, and Jackson, "Intensities."

15. For some very elementary models of this process, see Edwin T. Haefele, "A Utility Theory of Representative Government," *American Economic Review* vol. 61, no. 3 (June 1971), pp. 350–367. Froman, in *Congressman*, makes some observations which parallel this discussion, particularly on pp. 6 and 10.

16. *Ibid.*, p. 362.

17. Jerome Rothenberg, "A Model of Economic and Political Decision-Making," in J. Margolis, ed., *The Public Economy of Urban Communities* (Washington, D.C.: Resources for the Future, 1965).

18. John C. Wahlke, Heinz Eulau, William Buchanan, and Leroy C. Ferguson, *The Legislative System: Explorations in Legislative Behavior* (New York: John Wiley and Sons, 1962), pp. 272–276.

19. Matthews and Stimpson, "Decision-Making," p. 8.

20. Austin Ranney, *The Doctrine of Responsible Party Government: Its Origin and Present State* (Urbana: University of Illinois Press, 1954).

21. Warren E. Miller and Donald E. Stokes, "Constituency Influence in Congress," *American Political Science Review*, vol. 57, no. 1 (March 1963), p. 45.

22. Willmoore Kendall and George W. Carey, "The 'Intensity' Problem and Democratic Theory," *American Political Science Review*, vol. 62, no. 1 (March 1968), p. 19.

23. Edwin T. Haefele, "Environmental Quality as a Problem of Social Choice," in Allen Kneese and Blair Bower, eds., *Environmental Quality Analysis* (Baltimore: Johns Hopkins Press, 1972).

24. There is an important distinction here in the term *constituency* as used in the model describing how legislators *do* vote and as used in the discussion of how they *should* vote. In the descriptive model, the relevant constituency for representatives desiring reelection is confined to those people who will, or are likely to, vote in subsequent elections. The models of how legislators should vote if there is to be the desired correspondence between public policies and individual attitudes require that all people vote, or at least all who have an interest in the outcome of the election. The two definitions of constituency are not always the same given the de jure and de facto restrictions which various governments have placed on registration, such as residency requirements, poll taxes, and outright discrimination against groups of potential voters.

25. Arthur Maass, "System Design and the Political Process: A General Statement," in Arthur Maass et al., *Design of Water Resource Systems* (Cambridge: Harvard University Press, 1962), p. 569.

26. *Ibid.*, pp. 569–571. Maass takes the first quote from Ernest Barker, *Reflections on Government* (London: Oxford University Press, 1942), pp. 41–42.

27. See earlier discussion and note 17.

28. Burns, *Deadlock*, chap. 14, proposes several reforms of this type designed to weaken the influence of individual districts. His hope is to make legislators more responsive to the national leadership.

29. See Julius Turner, "Responsible Parties: A Dissent from the Floor," *American Political Science Review*, vol. 45, no. 1 (March 1951), pp. 143–152, for an argument of this type.

30. Burns, *Deadlock*.

2. A MODEL OF LEGISLATIVE VOTING BEHAVIOR

1. These committee liberal and committee conservative variables are similar to Matthews and Stimpson's inclusion of the positions of the leaders of the Democratic Study Groups and the Conservative Coalition in their cue source model of House voting. Donald R. Matthews and James Stimpson, "Decision-Making by U.S. Representatives: A Preliminary Model," paper

presented at the Conference on Political Decision-Making, Lexington, Ky., April 10–11, 1968.

2. Donald R. Matthews, in *U.S. Senators and Their World* (Chapel Hill: University of North Carolina Press, 1960), pp. 216 and 252, gives conflicting predictions about the influence a senior member may have on the junior partner. He does predict that freshmen senators may be more dependent upon this information source. He and Stimpson also use a similar variable in their simulation of House voting, although in this case it is a state delegation variable. Matthews and Stimpson, "Decision-Making."

3. Truman specifically rejects the notion that the voting blocs uncovered in his study result from the systematic effects of similar constituencies. See David B. Truman, *The Congressional Party* (New York: John Wiley, 1959), pp. 164–166, 180, 191, 210–211, 217. Constituency is only used to account for conspicuous deviations from the party blocs. See pp. 69–71, 119.

4. *Ibid.*, pp. 289–308.

5. Donald R. Matthews and James A. Stimpson, "Decision-Making."

6. Warren E. Miller and Donald E. Stokes, "Constituency Influence in Congress," *American Political Science Review*, vol. 57, no. 1 (March 1963).

7. Duncan MacRae, Jr., with Fred Goldner, *Dimensions of Congressional Voting* (Berkeley: University of California Press, 1958), appendix C.

8. Miller and Stokes, "Constituency Influence," p. 19.

9. The simple correlation between state competitiveness and constituency influence may not be positive, however. It is possible that senators with low constituency coefficients will face the strongest challengers and be involved in the closest elections. Or, put simply, the best way for senators to have safe seats is to vote with their constituents. This would lead to a negative correlation between competitiveness and constituency influence. Given these countervailing forces, it is not clear what value the simple correlation between these two variables would have.

10. In this coalition model, the senate is a non-zero sum, *n*-person, cooperative game. Game theorists have not been successful at developing predictive models for this type of game.

11. Evans and Novak argue that Lyndon Johnson, when he was majority leader, engineered precisely this trade on the Civil Rights Act of 1958 when he got Senator Church of Idaho to vote for a jury trial amendment favored by southern senators in exchange for southern support for the Snake River project, which had been one of Church's campaign promises. Roland Evans and Robert Novak, *The Exercise of Power* (New York: New American Library, 1966), pp. 129–130.

12. Miller and Stokes, "Constituency Influence," p. 53.

3. MEASURING SENATE VOTING BEHAVIOR

1. See H. Douglas Price, "Are Southern Democrats Different?" in Nelson Polsby, Robert Dentler, and Paul Smith, eds., *Politics and Social Life* (Boston: Houghton Mifflin, 1963), pp. 740-756; Lee F. Anderson, Meredith Watts, Jr., and Allen R. Wilcox, *Legislative Roll Call Analysis* (Evanston: Northwestern University Press, 1966), chap. 6; and Duncan MacRae, Jr., *Issues and Parties in Legislative Voting* (New York: Harper and Row, 1970), chap. 2.

2. Louis Guttman, "The Quantification of a Class of Attributes: A Theory and Method of Scale Construction," in Paul Horst et al., *The Prediction of Personal Adjustment* (New York: Social Science Research Council, 1941), and Samuel A. Stouffer et al., *Measurement and Prediction* (Princeton: Princeton University Press, 1950).

3. This use of Guttman scales simply to assess legislators' position on specific bills is a departure from the traditional applications of Guttman scaling to roll call analysis. Previous studies have tried to use scales comprised of votes on many different bills to determine the number and content of issue dimensions underlying congressional voting behavior. The objective is to get as many bills as possible into a single, generalized scale such as social welfare, and still preserve the ordered and cumulative properties of the scale. See Duncan MacRae, Jr., *Dimensions of Congressional Voting* (Berkeley: University of California Press, 1958), and his *Issues and Parties in Legislative Voting* (New York: Harper and Row, 1970), chap. 2.

4. To handle the problem that all the scales did not have the same number of categories, the scales were standardized to a range of 0 to 4 with zero being the most conservative position, i.e., voting to limit the legislation as much as possible, in all cases. This range was selected because it constituted the modal number of groupings in the original scales. It also offered the best trade-off between the desirability of having a large number of groupings and the disadvantage of having to deal with bills with fewer than this number of groups.

Those scales which had fewer than five categories were inflated to the zero to four range by multiplying each score by four divided by the scale value of the highest category. Thus, if a scale had only four categories, they were scored as 0, 1.33, 2.67, and 4.00. On scales with more than five categories, the categories with the fewest frequencies were added to the adjacent larger groupings and the categories rescored. This aggregation was continued until there were five groups, scored 0 to 4. A table showing the original distributions by scale score and the rescaled distributions is included as Appendix 3.2 to this chapter.

5. Henrietta Poynter and Nelson Poynter, *Congressional Quarterly Almanac* (Washington, D.C.: Congressional Quarterly, 1961), vol. 17 (1961), p. 621.

6. These results provide a small amount of external validation for the scales. The fact the president's behavior fit the previously defined scale patterns indicates that a person knowledgeable about the legislation, yet outside the Senate, ranked the amendments in an order similar to the scaling procedure.

7. The justification of the use of demographic and regional characteristics to proxy relative constituency opinions has been stated by MacRae as, "What we must investigate, if we are concerned with the connection between representatives and their constituencies, is the degree of association between roll-call votes and constituency characteristics. If this association is high, we infer that in some way the constituencies have influenced the legislators . . . For if the association is high, the representative may be said to represent relatively local interests, and this in itself has significance for the functioning of representative government." MacRae, *Dimensions*, p. 256. Demographic variables, and presumably this justification, have also been used by J. Turner, *Party and Constituency* (Baltimore: Johns Hopkins Press, 1951), Lewis A. Froman, Jr., *Congressmen and Their Constituents* (Chicago: Rand McNally, 1963), Cleo H. Cherryholmes and Michael J. Shapiro, *Representatives and Roll Calls* (Indianapolis: Bobbs-Merrill, 1969).

8. The FAP example given in Appendix A suggests that even after the Voting Rights Acts, southern Democratic senators were less sensitive to blacks in their constituencies than are other senators.

9. The precise form of the estimated relationship between the constituency characteristics and senators' votes is a nonlinear one. It is hypothesized that senators' voting behavior is more sensitive to differences in these constituency characteristics near the middle of their range—50 percent for a variable expressed as a percentage, for example—than for equal difference near the extremes. In other words, there will be greater differences in the voting behavior of a senator from a state with 35 percent of its population in urban areas and one from a state with 65 percent of its population in urban areas than there will be between the first senator and a third representing a state with only a 5 percent urban population. The log-reciprocal model discussed by Johnston is used to model this hypothesis. See J. Johnston, *Econometric Methods* (New York: McGraw-Hill, 1963), pp. 49–50. The general multivariate form for this model is

$$\log_e V = b_0 - \frac{b_1}{z_1} - \frac{b_2}{z_2} - \ldots - \frac{b_n}{z_n}$$

where V represents the senators' scale scores and the Z's are the demographic variables. This form for the constituency models also fits the observed distribution of scale scores, which showed a large number of 0 and 4 scores, better than a linear relationship.

10. An interesting way to evaluate the constituency models is by the amount of variance in voting behavior which can be explained by these characteristics. The coefficient of determination (R^2) ranged from 0.220 for the National Wilderness Preservation to 0.895 for extending the Civil Rights Commission. The civil rights issues, as a group, had by far the highest explained variance. This result is consistent with the study by Miller and Stokes analyzing the votes of House members on civil rights in 1958. They found a high correlation between constituency attitudes and the representative's perception of them and between their perception and their roll call behavior. These correlations were higher for civil rights than for the social welfare and foreign policy issues included in the study. Warren E. Miller and Donald E. Stokes, "Constituency Influence in Congress," *American Political Science Review*, vol. 57, no. 1 (March 1963). Only three bills—the Cultural Exchange Program, the National Wilderness Preservation, and Comsat—had an explained variance below 30 percent.

11. Comparisons of this type, both within each senator's equation and among senators, require that all the explanatory variables be measured accurately. This is one of the assumptions of the statistical procedures. For example, if a senator's constituency variable is an erroneous measure of constituency position on each bill and these errors are random across bills, while the leader variables are accurately measured, the statistical techniques will underestimate the influence of constituency and possibly overestimate the leader's influences. See J. Johnston, *Econometric Methods*, pp. 148–150, for a discussion of this problem. However, as Appendix A shows, the procedures followed here introduce systematic errors into the constituency variables which may lead to overestimates of constituency influences. In the simulation in this appendix, the estimated coefficients were highly correlated with the actual influence of each variable. If this is also true for the senate, then comparisons should be meaningful.

12. The precise procedure used for the simultaneous equations was two-stage least squares. See J. Johnston, *Econometric Methods*, pp. 258–260.

13. There are a series of econometric arguments that even in the case of a series of nonsimultaneous equations, ordinary regression may not be the best method due to correlations among the error terms in the various equations. These arguments are acknowledged here. However, the technique involved is too complicated (and expensive) for use with the models and data presented here. See Arnold Zellner, "An Efficient Method of Esti-

mating Seemingly Unrelated Regressions and Tests For Aggregation Bias,"
Journal of the American Statistical Association, 57:348–368 (June 1962).

4. VOTING BEHAVIOR OF INDIVIDUAL SENATORS

1. Statistical significance was measured by the t-statistic computed for
each coefficient under the null hypothesis that the coefficient was zero. The
variables whose coefficients had very low t-statistics were the ones deleted
from the second set of estimations to get an equation with only significant
coefficients.

2. Any negative coefficients estimated for the organizational variables
should be viewed cautiously given the problems discussed in Appendix A.
Consequently, they will be omitted from the discussion but are shown in
each table for completeness. The only exception to this is the presidential
coefficients, which could be negative for Republicans and possibly some
southern Democrats.

3. These results are consistent with those presented in an earlier paper, in
which I tried to construct similar constituency only models for five bills
from the 81st and 83rd Congresses. See J. Jackson, "Some Indirect Evi-
dences of Constituency Pressures on the Senate," *Public Policy*, 14:253–270
(1967). These models fit much better for the nonincumbent party, the
Republicans during the 81st and the nonsouthern Democrats in the 83rd.
I suggested that for the party in control of both the presidency and the
Senate, the formal leaders' influence is greater, and consequently the constituency influence explains less of senators' voting behavior. James Sundquist
offers a similar interpretation (interview, The Brookings Institution, Washington, D.C., March 13, 1968). He maintains that the 1961–1962 sessions of
the Senate were not the most interesting to study because most Democratic
senators were supporting President Kennedy's positions and the votes of
Mansfield and Humphrey essentially coincided with the administration's
positions. Although this is an oversimplified hypothesis, for Mansfield's and
Humphrey's votes were not identical, it indicates that Mr. Sundquist believes
that the Kennedy administration was unusually influential and worked
through the Democratic leaders in the Senate.

4. Interview with Sam Merrick, Institute of Politics, Harvard University,
Cambridge, Mass., November 1967.

5. David B. Truman, *The Congressional Party* (New York: John Wiley,
1959), pp. 106 and 115, and pp. 205–206 (for the House).

6. A variable measuring the mean position of only the northern Democrats
was also tried in Mansfield's equation. This variable had about the same size
coefficients as the mean Democrat variable but a larger standard error.

7. Truman, *Congressional Party*, pp. 282.

8. *Ibid.*

9. See note 3.

10. Donald R. Matthews, *U.S. Senators and Their World* (Chapel Hill: University of North Carolina Press, 1960), pp. 216, 252.

11. It is easy to show the difference in the structural and reduced form equations. If Hill's votes are a function of the Alabama constituency and Sparkman's positions and Sparkman's are a function of Hill's and the committee chairman's, each structural equation is written as

$$\text{Hill} = a_{11} + a_{12} \text{ Alabama} + a_{13} \text{ Sparkman} + e_1$$

$$\text{Sparkman} = a_{21} + a_{22} \text{ Committee Chairman} + a_{23} \text{ Hill} + e_2.$$

The reduced form equations express both senators' votes as a function of Alabama and Committee Chairman, the exogenous variables.

$$\text{Hill} = b_{11} + b_{12} \text{ Alabama} + b_{13} \text{ Committee Chairman} + u_1$$

$$\text{Sparkman} = b_{21} + b_{22} \text{ Alabama} + b_{23} \text{ Committee Chairman} + u_2.$$

The coefficients in these reduced form equations, the b's, measure the total change in each senator's positions associated with a change in the positions of the constituency or the committee chairman.

12. V. O. Key, Jr., *Southern Politics* (New York: Knopf, 1949), pp. 359–360.

13. Ralph K. Huitt, "The Outsider in the Senate: An Alternative Role," *American Political Science Review*, vol. 55, no. 3 (Sept. 1961), p. 569.

14. Truman, *Congressional Party*, p. 101.

15. Interview with Stephen Horn, The Brookings Institution, March 15, 1968. Mr. Horn is a former administrative assistant to Senator Kuchel.

16. This observation strongly suggests that the high weights Matthews and Stimpson obtained for the congressman's state delegation variables result from their omission of all constituency variables. The members of each party from a single state are very likely to be representing similar constituencies and receiving similar constituency pressures. Had Matthews and Stimpson included a constituency variable and used a multivariate technique to estimate their simulation, they likely would have obtained lower state delegation weights. See Donald R. Matthews and James A. Stimpson, "Decision-Making by U.S. Representatives: A Preliminary Model," paper presented at the Conference on Political Decision-Making, University of Kentucky, Lexington, Ky., April 10–11, 1968.

17. Interview with William Gibbons, formerly with the Senate Democratic Policy Committee and legislative specialist with the Agency for the International Development, Washington, D.C., March 15, 1968.

5. ESTIMATES OF 1963 VOTING BEHAVIOR

1. Senator McCarthy's votes could not be estimated because Senator Kerr, who died between Congresses, was included in McCarthy's equation. Similarly, Gore's and Yarborough's votes were partially a function of Kefauver's positions, and thus their positions could not be predicted after Kefauver's death.

2. In a few cases, the estimated scale values were greater than 4 or less than 0 and thus outside the range of the actual scales. In these instances, the values were changed to 4 and 0 respectively.

3. The term $(1-U^2)$ is used in spite of its awkwardness because it is an adaption of the U^2 statistic discussed by Theil. See Henri Theil, *Applied Economic Forecasting* (Chicago: Rand McNally, 1966), pp. 26–29. The precise formula for the $(1-U^2)$ statistic is

$$(1-U^2) = 1 - \frac{\displaystyle\sum_{j=1}^{25} (V_{i,j} - P_{i,j})^2}{\displaystyle\sum_{j=1}^{25} (V_{i,j} - \bar{V}_i)^2}$$

where $P_{i,j}$ = Predicted score for senator i on bill j

$V_{i,j}$ = Actual score for senator i on bill j

$\bar{V}_i$ = Mean actual score of senator i on 1963 scales.

The comparison with the R^2 is clear. The formula for R^2 is

$$R^2 = 1 - \frac{\Sigma\, e_j^2}{\Sigma\,(Y_j - \bar{Y})^2} = 1 - \frac{\Sigma\,(Y_j - \hat{Y}_j)^2}{\Sigma\,(Y_j - \bar{Y})^2}$$

where $\hat{Y}_j$ is the value of Y_j predicted by the regression equation.

4. The estimated standard deviation of the prediction errors, referred to as the root mean squared error (RMSE), is simply the square root of the sum of the squared prediction errors. The estimated standard deviation of the error terms in the 1961–62 equations, referred to as the standard error of the estimate (SE), is part of the basic output of most regression analyses. The standard error of the estimate is simply the square root of the sum of the squared residuals (estimation errors) divided by the number of observations (T) minus the number of estimated coefficients (K),

$$s = \sqrt{\frac{\sum_{t=1}^{T} (Y_t - \hat{Y}_t)^2}{(T-K)}}$$

See J. Johnston, *Econometric Methods* (New York: MacGraw-Hill, 1963), p. 112.

5. This goes counter to the hypotheses of Matthews, who predicted that senators up for reelection will be more likely to vote with the party leaders. Donald R. Matthews, *U.S. Senators and Their World* (Chapel Hill: University of North Carolina Press, 1960), pp. 136–137.

6. See Chapter 2.

7. George MacGregor Burns, *The Deadlock of Democracy* (Englewood Cliffs, N.J.: Prentice-Hall, 1963).

8. Arthur M. Schlesinger, Jr., in *A Thousand Days* (Boston: Houghton Mifflin, 1965), p. 973, describes this reaction as it affected the House.

9. Stated formally, the method used to test for possible influence shifts required reestimating senators' 1961–62 voting model with the 1961–63 data and a complete set of dummy variables. If a senator's 1961–62 equation was:

$$\text{Vote}_{1961\text{-}62} = a_1 + a_2 \text{ Constituency} + a_3 \text{ Mansfield} + a_4 \text{ Committee Chairman},$$

the new model estimated was

$$\text{Vote}_{1961\text{-}63} = a_1 + a_2 \text{ Constituency} + a_3 \text{ Mansfield} + a_4 \text{ Committee Chairman} + b_1 D + b_2 (D * \text{Constituency}) + b_3 (D * \text{Mansfield}) + b_4 (D * \text{Committee Chairman}) + b_5 (D * \text{President}),$$

where D is a dummy variable which equals zero for the thirty-six 1961–1962 observations, and one for the twenty-five 1963 observations. The implication of this second equation is that the a coefficients measure the influence of each variable in 1961–62 and the b coefficients measure how this influence changed between 1961–62 and 1963. The estimated influence of each variable in 1963 is the sum of the appropriate a and b coefficients. The ratio of each b coefficient and its standard error is a conventional test of the null hypotheses that $b = 0$, or that there was no change in the influence of the particular variable. It is unlikely that all the coefficients would change, however. Consequently, the equation containing the dummy variables was estimated a second time, deleting the particular dummy variables where there was no apparent change in a variable's influence.

6. VOTING BEHAVIOR ON SPECIFIC LEGISLATION

1. The formula for the $(1-U^2)$ statistic in the comparisons in this chapter is the same formula outlined in note 3, Chapter 5, except that the predicted scale score from the appropriate naive model is substituted for the senator's mean scale score in the denominator of the expression.

2. See Warren E. Miller and Donald E. Stokes, "Constituency Influence in Congress," *American Political Science Review*, vol. 57, no. 1 (March 1963), and Lewis A. Froman, *Congressman and Their Constituencies* (Chicago: Rand McNally, 1963).

3. Roland Evans and Robert Novak, *The Exercise of Power* (New York: New American Library, 1966), pp. 129–130.

7. CONSTITUENCIES, LEADERS, AND PUBLIC POLICY

1. See H. D. Price, "Careers and Seniority in the 19th Century Congress," in William Aydelotte, ed., *Quantitative Studies and Legislative Behavior* (Princeton, N.J.: Princeton University Press, forthcoming) for a description of the development of the formal congressional party structures, seniority, and longer careers.

2. Donald R. Matthews, *U.S. Senators and Their World* (Chapel Hill: University of North Carolina Press, 1960), p. 127.

3. Arguments to this effect have been made by E. T. Haefele, "A Utility Theory of Representative Government," *American Economic Review*, vol. 61, no. 3 (June 1971), by Willmoore Kendall and George W. Carey, "The 'Intensity' Problem and Democratic Theory," *American Political Science Review*, vol. 62, no. 1 (March 1968), and by James S. Coleman, "The

Possibility of a Social Welfare Function," *American Economic Review*, vol. 56, no. 5 (Dec. 1966).

4. William Riker has argued that uncontrolled vote trading can go too far. See his "The Paradox of Vote Trading," paper presented at the Annual Meeting of the American Political Science Association, Washington, D.C., Sept. 6–9, 1972. However, E. T. Haefele's comments on Riker's paper, entitled "Paradox Lost," point out that various outcomes to Riker's example exist which are preferred by a majority of the members to both the no-trading and Riker's outcomes. Since all possible coalitions of the three members could reach this same point, no coalition could be stable, which makes the example similar to three people trying to divide a pie. Haefele's point is that potential coalitions exist which would stop the trading before it gets to Riker's point and that trading is beneficial. One of the roles for political parties and their leaders is to control the amount and extent of the trading in such situations.

5. One final caveat. The observations about the appropriateness of the representational and coalition models apply only to floor voting. As mentioned earlier, it is possible, even likely, that committee behavior does not fit this descriptive model. In that case, normative statements do not apply to committee decisions and thus to Congress as a whole. However, the fact that the coalition representational explanations fit floor behavior suggests possibilities for committee and floor reform.

6. Kendall and Carey, " 'Intensity Problem'."

7. E. T. Haefele, "Utility Theory," and "Environmental Quality as a Problem of Social Choice," in Allen Kneese and Blair Bower, eds., *Environmental Quality Analysis* (Baltimore: Johns Hopkins Press, 1972), and Jerome Rothenberg, "A Model of Economic and Political Decision-Making," in Julius Margolis, ed., *The Public Economy of Urban Communities* (Washington, D.C.: Resources for the Future, 1965).

8. For a discussion of the role of the legislature vis-à-vis administrative agencies at the local level, see John Jackson, " 'People or Ducks,' Who Decides?," in Allen Kneese and Edwin Mills, eds., *Economics of the Environment* (New York: National Bureau of Economic Research, forthcoming).

Index

Harvard Political Studies

*Out of print

*John Fairfield Sly. *Town Government in Massachusetts (1620–1930)*. 1930.

*Hugh Langdon Elsbree. *Interstate Transmission of Electric Power: A Study in the Conflict of State and Federal Jurisdictions*. 1931.

*Benjamin Fletcher Wright, Jr. *American Interpretations of Natural Law*. 1931.

*Payson S. Wild, Jr. *Sanctions and Treaty Enforcement*. 1934.

*William P. Maddox. *Foreign Relations in British Labour Politics*. 1934.

*George C. S. Benson. *Administration of the Civil Service in Massachusetts, with Special Reference to State Control of City Civil Service*. 1935.

*Merle Fainsod. *International Socialism and the World War*. 1935.

*John Day Larkin. *The President's Control of the Tariff*. 1936.

*E. Pendleton Herring. *Federal Commissioners: A Study of Their Careers and Qualifications*. 1936.

*John Thurston. *Government Proprietary Corporations in the English-Speaking Countries*. 1937.

*Mario Einaudi. *The Physiocratic Doctrine of Judicial Control*. 1938.

*Frederick Mundell Watkins. *The Failure of Constitutional Emergency Powers under the German Republic*. 1939.

*G. Griffith Johnson, Jr. *The Treasury and Monetary Policy, 1933–1938*. 1939.

*Arnold Brecht and Comstock Glaser. *The Art and Technique of Administration in German Ministries*. 1940.

*Oliver Garceau. *The Political Life of the American Medical Association.* 1941.

*Ralph F. Bischoff. *Nazi Conquest through German Culture.* 1942.

*Charles R. Cherington. *The Regulation of Railroad Abandonments.* 1948.

*Samuel H. Beer. *The City of Reason.* 1949.

*Herman Miles Somers. *Presidential Agency: The Office of War Mobilization and Reconversion.* 1950.

*Adam B. Ulam. *Philosophical Foundations of English Socialism.* 1951.

*Morton Robert Godine. *The Labor Problem in the Public Service: A Study in Political Pluralism.* 1951.

*Arthur Maass. *Muddy Waters: The Army Engineers and the Nation's Rivers.* 1951.

*Robert Green McCloskey. *American Conservatism in the Age of Enterprise: A Study of William Graham Sumner, Stephen J. Field, and Andrew Carnegie.* 1951.

*Inis L. Claude, Jr. *National Minorities: An International Problem.* 1955.

*Joseph Cornwall Palamountain, Jr. *The Politics of Distribution.* 1955.

*Herbert J. Spiro. *The Politics of German Codetermination.* 1958.

Harry Eckstein. *The English Health Service: Its Origins, Structure, and Achievements.* 1958.

*Richard F. Fenno, Jr. *The President's Cabinet: An Analysis in the Period from Wilson to Eisenhower.* 1959.

Nadav Safran. *Egypt in Search of Political Community: An Analysis of the Intellectual and Political Evolution of Egypt, 1804-1952.* 1961.

*Paul E. Sigmund. *Nicholas of Cusa and Medieval Political Thought.* 1963.

Sanford A. Lakoff. *Equality in Political Philosophy.* 1964.

*Charles T. Goodsell. *Administration of a Revolution: Executive Reform in Puerto Rico under Governor Tugwell, 1941-1946.* 1965.

Martha Derthick. *The National Guard in Politics.* 1965.

Bruce L. R. Smith. *The RAND Corporation: Case Study of a Nonprofit Advisory Corporation.* 1966.

David R. Mayhew. *Party Loyalty among Congressmen: The Difference between Democrats and Republicans, 1947-1962.* 1966.

Isaac Kramnick. *Bolingbroke and His Circle: The Politics of Nostalgia in the Age of Walpole.* 1968.

Donald W. Hanson. *From Kingdom to Commonwealth: The Development of Civic Consciousness in English Political Thought.* 1970.

Ward E. Y. Elliott. *The Rise of Guardian Democracy: The Supreme Court's Role in Voting Rights Disputes, 1845-1969.* 1974.

John E. Jackson. *Constituencies and Leaders in Congress: Their Effects on Senate Voting Behavior.* 1974.